ADULTING DOESN'T HAVE TO SUCK! #2

You Can Do This!

Climb over the mountain of work and slide down the hill of house cleaning. Ski across the chaos in the kitchen and pull the rope that guides you through the swamp of all the things you keep forgetting.

Along the way Adulting Doesn't Have To Suck! #2 will help you discover a plethora of ideas to make tiny changes in your life.

And when you reach the other side, you'll find a rainbow of fun times and good friends waiting for you to stop stressing out and have some fun. You can do this!

ADULTING DOESN'T HAVE TO SUCK! #2

More Tips From An
Organized Mom

Pat Sawtelle

Adulting Doesn't Have To Suck! #2

© 2020 by Pat Sawtelle. All rights reserved.

Cover Design by Sheri McGathy

No part of this book may be reproduced, copied, scanned, or transmitted in any form, by any means, electronic, mechanical, photocopying, recording, or otherwise without written permission from the author.

This book is a collection of things Pat Sawtelle learned in life. All the information is simply ideas and you should consult experts in the appliable fields to keep updated on current laws, science, and recommendations.

All brand names and product names used in this book are trademarks, registered trademarks, or trade names of their respective holders. Pat Sawtelle is not associated with any product or vendor in this book.

Published by CozyPar Publishing

Visit PatSawtelle.com to explore other novels and short stories from the author.

Library of Congress Control Number: 2021946940

ISBN: 978-1-955925-05-1 (hardcover)
ISBN: 978-1-955925-03-7 (paperback)

Dedication

I dedicate this book to my author, editor, and publisher friends who've inspired me, encouraged me, provided feedback, and shared their knowledge with me. This group of people welcomes new writers with open arms and is always willing to share what they've learned.

An extra-large hug to Kristi Bradley for taking on the editing of the Adulting Doesn't Have To Suck! books and putting up with my endless author questions over the years.

And if my magic wand starts working again, I'll use it to get readers to buy and write online reviews of all your books!

TABLE OF CONTENTS

THE TIPS CONTINUE 1

THE LAUNDRY ROOM 5

THE KITCHEN 15

THE BATHROOM 29

NOOKS AND CRANNIES IN THE HOME 45

LADIES WEAR ALMOST ANYTHING 55

THE WORLD OF MANLY CLOTHES 59

STORING YOUR WEARABLES 71

TRANSPORTATION 87

WORKING SMARTER 95

JOBS PAY THE BILLS 107

BUSINESS SOFTWARE TIPS 117

LIFE PLANS 125

END OF LIFE PLANNING 131

TRAINING YOUR BRAIN 139

LIFE LESSONS REVISITED 151

COOKING TO LIVE 167

WHERE YOU LIVE 181

IT'S ALL ABOUT YOU 191

PARTY TIME! 195

APPENDIX - HOW TO MAKE A BOX 201

THE TIPS CONTINUE

The first book is buttoned up and off to the publisher and I'm returning to life working and enjoying time with my family. However, my life has decided it doesn't like so much of my attention preferring I take time each day to continue my writings. So, sit back and get ready for another round of tips, ideas, explanations, and things to make you think.

Grab something to drink and take a few minutes to sit in your favorite room. Look at all you've learned, congratulate yourself on all the ways you've improved daily life. You've taken the first steps to coping with life as an adult, but there is a bit more work to do. From house cleaning to cooking, learning to jobs, the questions from the twenty somethings in my life haven't stopped.

Learning… I see you rolling those eyes and thinking I can't believe she went there. Digging your heals in and saying I am not in school and I refuse to go there again just indicates you have a bit more work to do on being an Adult!

Learning is a basic part of life even when you get out of school. Reading and using Adulting Doesn't Have to Suck! books is learning. Figuring out how to read the label on your favorite frozen pizza, or understanding those legal terms on the mattress financing contract is learning. In life you take tests when you apply the information to support your needs and an A means you understood the information and how to apply it successfully. (No, we don't have graded papers, but it's still a test.)

Remember This: Waste Not. Want Not.

This is a simple concept that should guide all parts of your life. From food or cleaning supplies, to items no longer needed, ask if you're wasting something before throwing it away. Use the last little bit at the bottom of the shampoo bottle to fully get your money out of it. Planning meals can reduce waste by using all the ingredients and cooking to fit the number of people you have to feed. Recycling plastic and glass will reduce the impact on landfills while saving natural resources. Selling or giving away clothes or furniture you no longer want reduces waste and opens up space in your home.

I'd like to take a moment to acknowledge those who live in rural communities, farms, or ranches. Your life style is all about not wasting. You have compost piles or pigs to feed, use glass and paper over plastic where possible, burn what you can, look for long term functionality on what you buy and make the rest of us look like slackers. (Hats off to you!) But even those individuals have things to learn, could use a few tips, and might need a few habit changes to make life better.

Life's sinister side throws challenges in your path every day waiting to see if you're up to the challenge. Those who say *bring it on* are willing to look at the challenge as an opportunity to learn something that will help them come out in a better place. Every one and every thing in your life should be considered a resource. From using that rolling suitcase to move things around the house, to doing internet searches and phoning family or friends, gathering information (learning… LOL) will help you succeed.

Okay, I through preaching now. But you get the point. Don't skip parts of the book because you think you don't need to know that stuff. Keep an open mind and mark parts that you'll need for later. Not everything will stay in your brain but you can remember you have a resource to find things on that topic.

I hope you find more useful and fun things in this book than you expect to read about. Share them with friends and post tips of your own. Enjoy making a few more changes in your life and see who takes notice. Those are people who really care about you. Be sure the thank them for taking notice.

Let's get started on the next round of things that might be helpful to your *adulting* life!

THE LAUNDRY ROOM

The laundry room is your friend. It makes things clean. However, doing laundry is high on the list of chores I don't like. Okay, fine. I'll admit it. I hate all chores, but this ranks at the top of the list of things I wish I had a magic wand to do for me. Mounds of dirty clothes for a family of four felt never-ending to me. I can't imagine doing it for more people. Coming up with a plan to tackle this along with everything else in my life while keeping my sanity took a bit. Here's what I learned over the years.

Don't wear so many clothes! Don't laugh… it's a valid solution to the volume. College friends taught me their process of analyzing the length of time I wore something. An hour or two for a dinner out rated a second-wear status. Workout clothes and last night's bar hopping outfit went immediately into the next load of wash. (That kept down the smells in the house.)

Germ adverse or people worried about neatness would always wash more clothes, but my friends had better things to do with their time in college than laundry. (Hey, it's a valid point even if I choose not to follow their sometimes *odoriferous* guidance.)

Here are a few easy tips to try.
- Read the labels BEFORE you buy clothes. If you don't like to wash, consider clothes you take to the dry cleaners. If you don't like, or can't afford, the dry cleaners, buy wash and wear fabrics.
- If you don't own an iron or know how to use one, watch out for those 100% cotton or linen fabrics that will probably need you to iron.
- That favorite cashmere sweater will only fit your toddler or teddy bear if you put it in the washer and dryer. Follow the cleaning instructions carefully!
- Cold water keeps colors from fading as fast and hot water can make some of them dull.
- Uniforms for the mechanical trades and maybe even the food industry are candidates for hot water to remove the chemicals and grime. Run these through with a slightly heavier dose of cleaner and an extra rinse cycle to give them a top-notch clean.
- Hook your bras closed when you take them off. This reduces the chances of them hooking onto other fabrics in the washer and dryer. Hook them on the row you don't use when you wear them to extend the life of the hooks on the back. Or stick them in one of those mesh laundry bags to keep them from getting tangled in other clothing.
- Open out your socks and untangle clothes before putting them in the laundry. This lets the washer do a better job of washing and the dryer for drying while making loading quicker.

Tip: Fix the tangles as you take clothes off before putting in the hamper, saving time later. And for goodness sakes empty out your pockets before you take them off.

- Lint gathering fabrics are everywhere and not easy to spot. Some clothes, especially black pants, attract fuzz. Be sure to wash those in a separate load from fuzzy items like towels and sweaters.
- Fold / hang clothes with the crease. If the pants have a fold down the middle of the front on each leg, be sure to fold with the crease for the best results. It's normally best to hang pants, but the creasing rule still goes.
- Drying items that cause a lot of lint like blankets, rugs and heavy clothing? Stop them halfway through and empty the lint trap. This will reduce the chances it will overflow into your dryer vent pipe and keep the proper airflow for drying efficiency. Shaking them out at the stop point will let the hot air reach new places as well.

Washers And Dryers Have Limits

Capacity can be the difference between three and eight towels in a load of laundry. The smaller washer and dryer that worked great for your single life won't keep up with your family or frat brothers. The newer model washers claim to spin more moisture out of fabric to save time on drying.

As of late, I see more consumers buying a model without that center agitator post saying it does less damage to your clothes. I also found that without the agitator, it lets me wash blankets and bedspreads. I discovered another improvement when it came time to get the clothes out. Nothing had tangled into that agitator column which also reduced the damage to my clothes.

If you're shopping for a new washer or dryer there are several things to consider.
- Be sure the dryer door will open without trapping you in a corner.
- At the store, put music on your phone and place it in the bottom of the washer then close the top. This will provide insight into the amount of noise you'll hear when in use.
- Try reaching the back of the bottom of the washer to be sure you can reach that last sock without falling inside.

Ah, Fresh and Soft

Don't grab stuff off the store shelf without checking the details on that laundry detergent and fabric softener you love to use. There are so many options from regular to high efficiency, then you have a variety of scents and cleaning powers that claim to make it all perfect.

If you're on special water systems or drain systems you might have to use something compatible with those and it could limit your choices. Like many things in life, some people are allergic to certain brands or smells, and as we covered in the first Adulting Doesn't Have To Suck! book, these things impact your personal smell. Do a bit of shopping even trying a few brands to decide what works best for you and your clothes.

Read the instructions on your washer to confirm if you need regular or HE (high efficiency) detergents for those new washers. If you use powdered cleaners and notice dots of discoloration on your clothes, you have "hot spots". These are places were the detergent didn't spread out in the water concentrating too much cleanser on your clothes. The solution is easy. Switch to liquid and / or follow those washing instructions more carefully.

> **Tip.** If your machine doesn't have a special dispenser, put liquid detergent in the bottom before you add the clothes. This allows it to get into the holes at the bottom of the machine and mix with the water as it

fills the machine. That means all the items, including those on the bottom, get soap and not just the one favorite shirt on the top of the load where you poured in the detergent before slamming the lid shut.

Use the correct measurement of cleaner. If you overload the detergent the washer might not get all the soap out of the fabric.

Dryer sheets versus liquid softener in your washer is partially a personal preference normally based on what a family member or good friend taught you in the early years. However, the fabric care instructions from the clothing manufacturer also affect your selection. The purpose of fabric softener is to release wrinkles and reduce static in clothes and when used correctly it should not damage your clothing.

Most washers have a softener dispenser place for you to add the liquid so the machine will automatically add it at the correct cycle time. Remember too much of a good thing is bad for your clothes so don't heavy up on the softener.

Another option is the trusty dryer sheet. These don't require additional washing machine cleaning, but you do need to be sure they end up in the garbage and not on the floor. (Slip hazard.) For those using the sheets, even these can be a bit too much softener for those smaller loads or lighter fabrics. I found that tearing the sheets in half not only worked for all my various load sizes, it also made the box last twice as long. ($Money saving feature.)

More Laundry Tricks

When you take those wet clothes out of the washer, shake them out before putting them in the dryer. Shaking separates the fabric allowing the dryer to reach all the spots compressed during the wash cycle, reducing wrinkles in the dried clothing. It also uncovers some of those dollar bills you left in the pockets before you washed them. (Bonus!)

Using liquid softeners in the dispensing part of the washer requires periodic cleaning to keep it from stopping up with this thick solution. Check the instruction book on your washer for information on the cleaning timing and process. (Can't find it in the mess? Look online. Most instruction manuals are now only a quick search away)

At the very least, periodically wipe out the buildup even running some clean warm water through that spot to freshen it up. Yes, this option just added to that chores list so you might want to consider the other softener options.

At least once a month when you're ready to wash one of those loads of washcloths and towels, wet part of one. Then quickly wipe off the top of the washer and dryer. Lift the washer lid and wipe the inside of it and the surface around the softener dispenser and corners. Then drop it in with the wash.

If you don't like the thought of cleaning with a dirty towel, just use your preferred reusable cleaning cloth and place it in the laundry with the towels. Yes, you can use a paper towel, but if you're watching your pennies, save that for other things and stick with reusable options.

If you don't keep these areas neat, they build up dirt and grime that gets on your clean clothes. Do you want to wash things twice or make a one-minute cleaning swipe?

Revenge Of The Dryer

If you value your life and home, pay attention to the lint filter and build a safety habit now! A dryer works by tumbling your clothes around in hot air. During the process, small fibers separate from the clothes. This is called lint.

The dryer filter builds up with lint stopping air from flowing out of your dryer not only making it harder for your dryer to work it can make the unit get to hot damaging the equipment. When the filter is too full, it can also push the lint into the dryer vent pipe with results that aren't always great.

If you have a pipe that takes the air straight outside without any turns, it might just end up on the ground outside creating the need to clean up the mess, but little bits can hang out in the pipe as well. If your pipe turns up toward the roof or down from a second floor, the lint builds up in the pipe section closer to the dryer.

The dryer lint hung in the roof style pipe and caught fire, nearly costing one of my family members their house. Thankfully they smelled the smoke and put it out. (Fire extinguishers are an important item in every home.)

When your clothes take longer than normal to dry, be sure you've emptied the lint catcher. Air flow is critical to the drying process. When drying fluffy stuff stop the load half way through the drying cycle and empty the filter doing it again at the end. You'll find the item drying in a bit less time.

I recommend emptying the filter before you take out the clothes. If you get caught up in folding and putting away, or are interrupted by life in general, you might forget to empty the filter. Don't lose your home and favorite stuff over an easy habit.

> **Tip**: When moving into a home where others lived before you, either clean out the dryer vent or pay to have it done. This picture is what came from my son's dryer vent after they moved into an older home. It had the roof style dryer vent. Not only did their clothes take forever to dry, but it also damaged their dryer and put them in danger of a fire.

THE KITCHEN

Cooking, eating, or hanging out with family, the kitchen is home central. Some of my favorite memories are my children and their friends laughing in my kitchen on a weekend night. But for all the fun memories this room holds, it is the source of a lot of work. With a few ideas and a couple of good habits, the kitchen might become your favorite room, too.

Don't cook? Wait! Don't skip this section. This is not all about cooking. It's about making life easier. Kitchens shouldn't be scary places for anyone and I'm here to help you learn to love this room.

Do you find cooking challenging then get depressed at the mess? There are lots of ways to cook including takeout, microwaving, or using pans and utensils. You can learn even if it's just basics. Watch videos online, attend a class, follow a recipe, or even have a friend or beloved family member teach you. Then surprise them with tips from this chapter to show them you have skills in the kitchen, too.

Anyone can use tips on managing life in the kitchen. Buying basics on necessities like paper towels, cleaning supplies, and can goods in bulk to save money and trips to the store, is only a good idea if you have space to store the extras. Sometimes buying in bulk can back fire especially if you have to keep them on the kitchen counter because you don't have a place out of site to keep the extras.

> **Tip:** Once a year check all the cans and boxes in the pantry to be sure none of them have expired. If any cans are bowed out where they should be flat or round, throw them away! Do not be tempted to open them. The food inside is probably unsafe to eat. Opening the can releases dangerous germs that you don't want hanging around.

Let's slide into the kitchen on that spilled bottle of cooking oil (fun and dangerous) and look for things that will help you.

> **Tip:** If you just spilled some oil on the floor to try out the slide, imagine me shaking my head at your lack of thinking. Okay, let's clean up that cooking oil spill in two steps. First wipe the bulk up with paper towels. Then use a bit of your dishwashing liquid to wash the area and get the rest of it cleaned up. (And promise you won't do that again!)

Cook, Eat, Clean...Relax

The first rule of survival in the kitchen is that the dishwasher is your friend. Okay, so once they're clean you have to unload it, but it beats washing every dirty thing by hand, drying, and putting it away after every meal or leaving the sink filled with dirty dishes that will smell up the kitchen.

Put everything you can in the dishwasher. Don't make a short stop and leave it in the sink as that makes two steps out of the process instead of one. When it's full, add soap and let it do the cleaning.

There are a few tips for loading the dishwasher.
- Glasses must be loaded upside down to let the water shoot inside them from below.
- Knives go down in the basket to reduce the opportunity for cuts, but forks and spoons have their handles on the bottom of the basket so the spray hits the eating area.
- There has to be space between the bowls and plates if you want the water to get them clean.
- If you aren't running the machine after every meal, I recommend a quick rinse of the items before loading them in the dishwasher. This allows you to run the machine on the regular setting instead of heavy-duty to remove caked-on leftovers.
- If you notice a not so clean smell in the dishwasher look for a "build-up of stuff" where the bottom of the door meets the inside and around the other outer gaskets. Take a minute

to clean and the smells should go away. If not, you might have a drain problem that needs checking.

Cleanser options include basic powders, detergent balls, and enhanced drying solutions. I recently saw a discussion where someone protested the use of the dishwasher because of the chemicals that touched the same surface as the next meal. I see the point, but washing them in the sink still uses a chemical. These chemicals are important for killing off the germs that could also make you sick. Pick your cleaning products carefully and don't leave them where small children can reach them.

Dishwashers can also clean mixing bowls, pots, and pans, but may require other settings to complete the task effectively. If you're using any of the new enhanced cleaning products, check the label for warnings on usage to prevent damage. Be cautious about putting your pots and pans in the dishwasher. Over time it can damage the handles.

I'll leave you to figure out your personal product preferences for the dishwasher. Just be sure to use hot water to improve cleaning and germ-killing. I use the basic powder and find it easy to reload the dispenser when I am through unloading the last clean load. That makes it easy to push the button on the way through the kitchen before I go to work when the washer is full.

For years, people in my house hesitated to open the dishwasher because they were afraid of putting dirty dishes in with the clean ones. I solved this with a wooden letter and some self-sticking magnets from the craft store. In our house, the letter "C" stands for both clean and caution. Clean so you know that if the dishwasher has shut off the dishes are clean. Caution because the family rule is, "if you open the clean dishwasher you have to unload it." When we turn on the machine, we put the letter on the front of the door. When someone unloads the washer, they put the "C" back on the counter. No more guessing or second washings.

If you don't like dishwashers or don't have one in your house, then don't let those dishes pile up in the sink for days building up that funky, smelly water and film on things. Remember that funky water and dried on food attracts bugs that results in another chore - pest control. So, make a point of cleaning dishes at least once each day to keep it in the short task realm and not the "I'll be here forever" list. They smell clean, the kitchen smells clean, and it keeps the kitchen neat. And when you're hungry, clean dishes mean you can find a plate to put food on. (Yep. I went there.)

For my take out only friends, be sure you throw away the trash after each meal. Don't leave the empty containers sitting around smelling up the place. If your town has recycling, be sure you know which containers can be recycled and rinse the plastic ones before putting them in the bin. (Many places don't recycle pizza boxes. Check your local rules.) And don't keep all those plastic to-go cups. You don't need fifty plastic cups. Recycle some or find a local school or crafting group that needs them. (Share the wealth.)

Be sure to change your washcloth or sponges and any drying or drain towels at least once or twice per week. Keep at least three to four sets so you can rotate as needed while washing the dirty ones. Some people prefer daily changes for cleaning fabrics for the ultimate low germ impact on their lives. If you prefer this plan, I recommend you buy about 10 to 12 sets. This lets you have a busy life week where you don't get to the laundry.

With a few minutes of attention after each meal the kitchen will stay clean ready to welcome you and your friends to come inside and enjoy the wonderful tastes awaiting your attention.

Small Things. Big Impact

Little tips for the kitchen can have a big impact on life. Dust and dirt take work and make food unhealthy. People prefer a kitchen that looks clean and tidy so they feel better about the food prepared in it.

Here are some additional tips for keeping the kitchen clean and functioning better.
- Keep glasses with the open end facing down in your cabinets to keep germs and dust from collecting on the inside.
- Keep a mop somewhere handy for spills, and of course to clean the floor every week or so.
- A broom and dustpan to clean up the stuff that fell off the counter used every few days can help reduce the need for mopping.
- Buy a garbage can with a lid to help your kitchen look tidy and trap the smells inside.
- Paper towels are great for counter spills, but if you're watching your money, keep a handy stack of kitchen cloths to wipe up the spill. Rinse these in the sink and toss in the washer to clean with the next load of laundry.
- Use department store pant clips to close and hang chip bags in a pantry.
- Do you have a pet that can take the lid off the plastic container with its food? Recycle one of those large holiday popcorn cans to seal them off. You can even spray paint the outside and decorate with permanent markers to personalize it for each of your pets. Don't paint

the inside. You don't want the food to touch the spray paint just to protect your pet.
- Freshen up the drain in the sink pouring in some Sprite or 7 Up to bubble away the odors.
- Run lemon or orange peels in the disposal to clean and make it smell good.
- Unclog a slow sink with vinegar and baking soda. Mix, pour, and let it sit for a while. It will also improve the smell.
- Keep noodles from boiling over by placing a wooden spoon across the pot or drop a teaspoon of cooking oil in the water. This keeps the stove cleaner when you cook reducing cleaning time.
- When heating in the microwave put the food in a circle leaving a hole in the middle like a donut to make it heat more evenly. Now the food stays in the container and not all over the walls and door of the microwave.
- During the heat of the summer, put leftover food bits in a used zip lock instead of directly in the trash. Freeze them until garbage day then drop in the can for trash pickup. This is great for things like shrimp, chicken, or fish that get a bit smelly in the trash and can stink up the kitchen.

Ewww… What's In Your Garbage Can?

The kitchen garbage can probably gets the most use in your home and traps the most smells. Be sure to buy the correct size bags and take it out at least once a week. If it begins to smell, don't wait to take it out immediately and reduce the funky odor in the kitchen.

Garbage bags come in both scented and unscented. I prefer the unscented because when people are in my kitchen, I want them to smell yummy food, not the perfume that I'll have to admit is the garbage can. Check the costs and weigh that against your odor preferences to determine what works for you.

From time to time, you need to let the garbage can air out for a few hours to keep the odors from building up inside creating the "I can't find that bad smell" spot. If the bag slipped or sprung a leak, be sure to hose out the can before relining. Putting a dryer sheet in the can bottom before you add the bag can also help with odors, but don't forget to replace it at least once a month throwing it and the smells out with the trash. If you don't have time for a good cleaning, then spray with something like Lysol and let it air out before relining.

Garbage Cans Aren't Just For Trash

Garbage cans come in all sizes and colors which gives you a list of other ways to use these handy containers. Many of these uses are best if you start with a new can as your old one might have lingering odors. If using an old can, be sure to take time to scrub it down before repurposing it.

Take two small plastic garbage cans like those that you would use in a bedroom or bathroom. Put them under a kitchen cabinet, in the pantry, or on / near the washer and dryer. Use one to throw dirty kitchen towels or cloths in to wait for the next laundry run. I keep it in the laundry room and add dirty socks found around the house or items with a pre-soak spray that needs to sit until I am ready to start the wash.

Use the second one to hold the plastic bags you get from the grocery or superstore. (Remember you can use these bags to line your small garbage cans around the house.) There's a plethora of other things these nifty small containers can hold. Corral those little chip and snack packages for lunches. Store your paper bags in one if you don't store them in a larger paper bag. Use a decorative version to hold magazines or extra towels in the bathroom. Let your imagination run with this one.

Since I regularly make dozens of Banana Nut Chocolate Chip Muffins, I use about 15 bags of pecans each year. (We buy them from a local charity fundraiser.) I stack the bags in a can slipping it under the bottom shelf in the pantry. The open bag is stored in a container in the freezer for easy use with the backup supply tucked out of the way.

Cooking For Necessity Or Pleasure

I'll admit I have a love-hate relationship with cooking. I can be good at it or fail miserably on any given day and frankly, these days I prefer writing to cooking. Yet I do enjoy a good meal and making it myself can be calming if I'm stuck in a writing project or family life decision.

Finding a happy place with the stove meant coming up with a few changes as my family size decreased with grown children. I can plan on feeding two or three for dinner to find I'm feeding ten and vice versa as they stop in for visits or rush off to live life.

Here are some ideas to make cooking easier.
- Making hamburgers. Get out your bottle of dish detergent (top open) before patting out that burger. Set it near the sink. With your hands covered in burger fat, you can now simply tip the bottle over with your forearm putting a few drops in your hand. Lather up then run under very warm water. Just like on your dishes it will cut through the grease with ease.
- Before you start cooking, empty the sink of any dirty dishes and prepare it with hot soapy water. As you finish with a bowl, utensil, etc., put in the water to soak until you are ready to wash.
- When chopping things like onions, bell peppers, celery, etc., always chop two to three times more than you need. Put the extra in small containers or baggies placing them in the freezer for use later on quick meal preparations.

- Keep a pad of paper and pen, or your Alexa / Google shopping list handy as you pull out ingredients. If you see the container is low, add it to the list. This keeps you from running out or having to search the cabinets before you go shopping.
- Soups, meatloaf, and chili are great items to prepare ahead in larger batches allowing you to freeze half to have for another meal the next week. Just save things in meal-sized microwave friendly containers before storing.
- Pick one day a week to cook several meals then pull one of them out of the refrigerator each night saving time when you get off work. Reheating is faster than full out cooking after a long day.
- Pick a night late in the week and declare it "Your choice night" or "leftover fun night". This is the night to pull everything out of the refrigerator and let the family choose what they want to eat. This means kids enjoy their favorites from the week and you reduce the volume of leftovers tucked in the back of the frig that needs to get thrown out.
- When stuffing pasta shells it is easier to do before they are cooked. Make your stuffing and put it in the uncooked shells. Place shells in a sauce with extra water or tomato juice. Cover and put in the refrigerator for twenty-four hours. The pasta will absorb the liquid. Then cook per the instructions.

THE BATHROOM

We have a love-hate relationship with the bathroom. It must provide a feeling of comfort to many of us while others demand luxurious accommodations that feel more like a palace. Generally, this is one of the smaller rooms in your home and may encompass an inner toilet or wet room within its expanse. Tile or carpet, shiny or nickel finish, bright colors or earth tones, all reflect the taste of the user and their desires. (If your bathroom is bigger than your kitchen you really need to rethink your priorities. Just saying!)

Only you can determine what you want, but let's put it in perspective. How much time per day do you spend in the bathroom for pleasure? I'm excluding your bubble bath time for this discussion. Remember if you are relaxing in the tub you have your eyes closed so think about that time only related to the bathtub and not the room.

Anyway, this is a room for showering, brushing teeth, putting on makeup, shaving, and of course necessary toilet time. You are in the room multiple times every day for brief periods and normally alone. Surrounding yourself in comfort includes good lighting, running water, properly working fixtures, and that hot water tank tucked away somewhere in the house. The color of the walls, carpets, and towels can be enough to start your day off on the wrong foot if you hate them, so these things are important.

Elevating this room into a luxury experience could include adding heated floors and towel racks, or toilets with warmers, music, or optional bidet (you know the thing that sprays your bottom with water.) Considering a bath or shower upgrade will offer you changes in the type and number of showerheads, or tubs with multiple massaging jets. The size of the tub and height of the shower spray is important, especially to those in the world who range on the bit taller side.

As you seek to define your personal bathroom design basics or luxury requirements, remember that upgrades could increase cleaning costs and / or maintenance to preserve a quality experience. Be sure your design choices are important to you and not a passing curiosity. For some of us, a smaller area with good lighting, pleasing colors, and properly functioning devices is all we want for those *stumble out of bed mornings* or late-night trips to the bathroom. For the rest of you, put it on the list of desires in your "fund me" list.

Here are some additional bathroom related topics that mom might have figured you picked-up on when you were living at home. Ask her if you want.

The Toilet Paper Roll

Don't you hate running out of toilet paper when your pants are down around your ankles and the next roll is across the room? Always keep a spare roll on the back of, or within arm's reach of, the toilet. When you put that roll on the holder, be sure the next one is in its place for easy reach or take a minute to refill the backup supply. This is simply a personal protection plan and cheaper than any embarrassment insurance you can buy if you could get it. I'm all about comfort and convenience.

Don't have a place near your toilet to store the roll? Get one of those paper towel holders from the kitchen and set it on the back of the toilet with three rolls on it. To plain looking for you? Put a baseball cap or the sports towel for your favorite team on top as a decoration.

Practical is not always fancy or girly. This solution keeps dust from gathering on the next roll ensuring a clean bum while adding style to those boring white rolls. If the cover gets dusty, toss it in with the next load of towels and replace it when clean.

While we're on the subject of toilet paper, do you know there are two ways to put on a roll and that people generally do it the same way each time? There is the over the top method and the underside option. Over the top simply means the paper hangs down in front of the roll. The underside puts the loose end near the wall. I recommend the over the top as you can find it a little easier if the paper is stuck to the roll. Think of it like a waterfall spilling toilet paper into your hand.

Want to have a bit of party fun? Ask which way people prefer to put on the roll and watch a lively discussion begin that will probably lead to other toilet passionate discussions including the seat up or down topic. When it comes to the bathroom, we take things seriously.

So why did I even bring this up? It's the picky details that you take care of which makes it easier not only to tear off the sheets but will make that special someone think you have a clue to life! Girls generally like a guy with habits that are compatible with the picky things their mom taught them, and this is one.

This goes for you guys as well. Impressing her can be so easy if you have the habits in place. Ladies, if a guy is into the details, you'll have to keep up to snag him. So, keep the extra roll on or near the toilet, put it on correctly, and never leave the bathroom with no paper on the dispenser roll! That could be grounds for some ugly words and might include a few health hazards.

Keeping The Toilet Clean

If you let the toilet stay dirty for too long, stains can set into the bowl and are hard to get out. Regular cleaning is important! If you don't have time to do it weekly consider using a bleach tablet in the tank. (That's the part at the top where you set the toilet paper, books or magazines, and has the handle for flushing.)

Wait! Am I getting too technical for some of you? Are you afraid of the toilet? Don't be. Let's back up and be clear about the parts of the toilet. If you understand what needs to be cleaned it takes out some of the fear. Only you can take out the gross. (This picture doesn't look very scary, but erasing a line will not clean the toilet!)

- If you have stains in the bowl part, start with a quick standard cleaning. Then flush. Now turn the water off at the wall and flush again keeping the water from filling the bowl again. Pour enough Coca Cola (use the bigger bottle) into the bowl to fill past the stain line. Let it sit, preferably overnight, then turn the water back on and flush. In many cases. this can reduce or remove a stain.
- Don't forget to clean the front of the bowl that slopes downward as well as where it meets the floor. This is the source of many bathroom odors.
- Remember to wipe off both sides of the seat lid. It's a great place to collect dust along with the base just behind where it attaches to the toilet bowl.

If you have a guest bathroom that doesn't get used very often, make a habit of using it at least once a week or at the very least flush it weekly to keep it fresh and reduce staining. (Unless you love to clean, that is.)

Aim...Fire...Wait. Where's The Seat?

The great bathroom controversy is, of course, does it matter if the seat is up or down, is the lid up or down, and includes, did the last person hit the target? Keep the seat down! Guys, this not only looks good to all ladies, including moms and sisters, but also hides the fact that you probably haven't hit the target nor cleaned the toilet recently. And ladies, this goes for you if you are not a "keep it clean" type of person. Think of this as self-defense for surprise visits from friends or mom!

Girls, you're usually not as picky about the lid as the seat. Most of you have a story about going in the middle of the night and falling in the water because a goofy brother left the seat up. Gentlemen, that one story will be the source of many fights with a girl and one that you can easily avoid with a bit of practice building a good habit. As far as the lid goes, if you have a lot of company or you're selling your home (appearance sells), always put the lid down too.

> **Tip:** Put the lid down before flushing to keep all the germs in the toilet instead of floating through the air getting yucky stuff on your toothbrush and counters.

Setting home sales aside, it also goes back to how clean is the appearance of your toilet. Dirty and lid down, just hope no one has to use it while visiting you. Clean and lid down who knows what they will think. Wonderful. Considerate. Outstanding. Impressive! If you're the visitor, put it down!

Now while we're in the bathroom, let's review a few tips that can reduce the amount of cleaning you have to do to look wonderful at all times. Always, always, hit the spot in the pot. If you miss, you need to clean more often because visitors don't always call before they come by.

A novel thought would be to stop and wipe up your miss when it happens. It might remind you to be more accurate in the future. If you're a visitor, hit it or clean it! No exceptions. And never, ever, leave a wet seat. No one wants to wipe up after you before they can use the toilet.

Secondly, keep a washable rug in front of the toilet to catch the drips and dirt your feet drag in. Then you can stuff the rug in the washer, hamper, or closet to keep the area neat at a moment's notice. If you invest in two rugs then a clean one is always ready to throw down for the ultimate clean image while the dirty one is hiding in the laundry hamper or washer. Again, a little practical advice and good habits make life and those first impressions so much easier.

Let's Talk Tubs And Showers

We take a shower or bath for several reasons. One is to relax as the hot water seeps into our body warming it to the bone. The second, and most important, is to get us clean. However, it is hard to feel clean if you are doing it in a dirty place. And the bathroom is one of those places that if you don't clean regularly, it gets harder to get it clean again. So, let's look at ways to make this easier and more enjoyable.

If you want that shower curtain to last longer and look better with less work, invest in the step-up version designed for commercial places. This style offers resistance to mold and mildew. Check your local discount superstore for one to use as a liner to your outer curtain or just dress the clear one up with great shower hooks. The clear curtains show soap scum, but they also open up the space making it feel larger, letting more light into the shower.

If you have a washer without the agitator in the middle (the curtain might not fit with an agitator), you might throw the liner in the wash with some vinegar every few months to cut some of the soap scum. Then just hang it back up to dry.

Always leave the inside curtain or liner spread open to dry after bathing or showering to keep the mildew from building up in the folds especially where it sticks to itself. In the long-run, this makes it look clean, longer, with less work, and of course, is cheaper than buying a new one every 6 months to stay ahead of mold and mildew. If you use the clear liner and no other curtains, you'll have fewer decorations to collect dust. Dusty fabrics require additional cleaning. However, keeping the decorator curtain clean is easily accomplished by putting them in the wash at least once a year.

Do you have the glass shower walls and doors? Many people say you should clean them thoroughly and then wax them every 6 months the way you wax your car. This is supposed to keep down on the build-up of soap scum. Do designers really think we have a love of waxing something we can't drive and show off? Reality is a bit different from the design world. Glass showers will build up a layer of soap scum! However, if you love waxing, an occasional wax job will help reduce the mess as long as you start waxing before you've used it. Waxing won't make the water and soap scum go away once they are on the surface.

For the rest of us, get the glass frosted to hide the scum and spray it with the best products you can find on the market that are designed to keep these items clean following the manufacturer's directions for usage. Once glass gets a soap scum layer, it's a lot of work to get it off. Unless, of course, you own a glass company and can just have it replaced every year or you're into some heavy-duty buffing and waxing.

- An old trick that came from one of my friends was to use a slightly wet old dryer sheet to scrub the glass on a shower door to remove soap scum. I think the dryer chemicals work a bit like waxing, but I'm not sure about this one.

You already spray cleaner on the shower walls at least once a month, don't you? No? Well, keep that mildew spray in easy reach of the bathroom. Then at least once a week, but not less than twice a month, as you get out of the shower, just spray the walls to keep them clean. Be aware of those runners or hinged areas that may need an extra squirt.

- Be sure you understand the manufacturer's instructions because if they say you need to wipe or rinse the product off after a few minutes you will need to do that to protect the finish on your shower.
- If it says to let sit and rinse, then spray before getting out of the shower, towel dry yourself, get dressed, and turn the shower on for a quick minute to wash away the chemical.
- Adding one of the spray attachments to a showerhead makes rinsing cleaners away even easier. If you don't have one of those keep a large plastic cup beside the spray bottle. Fill it up and splash on the parts you can't hit by moving the showerhead around.

Presto, an extra minute or two twice a month and you didn't need a lot of muscle to clean that shower. (Time saver!)

If you don't like standing in dirty water, you need to take care of the tub / shower drain. For those with longer hair simply brushing your hair before showering will remove many of the loose strands keeping them from building up in the drain catcher. Don't forget to wipe the hair from the drain cover after every shower or bath. Not only does it keep water flowing, it makes a good impression on others. With a bit of maintenance, you can save on drain cleaning bills.

Towels, Towels, Towels

Are you the kind who gets a new towel every time? Do you use yours for a week, or longer, before washing? Maybe you use it until it smells funny. There are a few basic pieces of information that can help you manage this important part of your personal hygiene routine.

One of the best parts of life is a hot shower followed with fresh smelling towels. Have at least two sets of towels and washcloths. Three or more is better for those one-time usage people! Wash the towels and washcloths at least weekly for ultimate freshness. Remember, good habits can bring extra benefits!

> **Tip:** Leave a small hand towel on the counter or on a hook near the sink for visitors to wipe their hands on. Guests don't want to dry their hands on your bath towel.

After you bathe/shower, if you leave the towel in the laundry hamper or on the floor when you're through using it, the area around it will begin to have that "wet" smell. Either put it straight into the washer or hang it up to dry out first. Hanging it up means the floor is tidy and there's no "wet smell" for visitors. And no towels on the floor also removes a tripping hazard.

Don't leave the washcloth wadded up on the side of the tub or shower shelf when you're through using it either. Just like the towel, it will smell and that takes away from the great feeling a shower brings you.

The shower and bath are other places with lots of bottles and stuff that can take away that peaceful feeling with clutter. Find something to hang on the wall to keep your shampoo bottles off the edge of the tub. Home organization companies make a variety of products to hang from the showerhead, suspend shelves from a rod, or baskets with suction feet for the wall. These generally have a place to hook a washcloth and even your razor, which is a bonus.

Wall hanger designs generally have holes in the plastic or are made of wire designs from shower friendly materials. This prevents trapping the water in the holder, which would create more cleaning work. These racks move things off flat surfaces making it easier to clean those areas. If it doesn't have hooks, just get a plastic suction hook for the wall to hang up that washcloth.

While shampoos and body soaps usually come in plastic bottles, your shaving creams don't. Be sure to put those metal cans on the wall or showerhead hanger and keep them off the sides of the tub or shower. This step prevents those wet cans from forming rust rings on the tub surfaces. Prevention beats buying a bunch of special cleaning products and a lot of heavy scrubbing time trying to remove that brownish-red stain.

NOOKS AND CRANNIES IN THE HOME

Homes have many little spots that get forgotten when cleaning but are always used to stash things in a hurry. In my home, any flat surface is considered fair game by the family to drop off anything in their hands at any time. These little bits get quickly forgotten leading to piles of stuff that never make it to their perfect place. Sigh… if only I could wave a magic wand and make them grow legs and walk to their correct place. (There I go dreaming again.)

Hall closets and linen closets capture things the family wants to deal with later or maybe hide so you never want them to move the things again. The plastic storage container cabinet in the kitchen looks like a seek and find puzzle. The wet bar has a flat surface that when not catching stuff doubles as a dust catcher. And these are just a few of the places that collect all kinds of things.

> **Bar Tip:** Cover shakers, bowls, and carafes with clear plastic wrap to keep off the dust between uses. This also goes for any pretty bowls you leave sitting out for that next party.

Don't roll your eyes and say that doesn't happen at your house. Go to any room and move your hand across all the flat surfaces. Anytime you encounter something that doesn't belong pick it up and put it where it goes. By the time you finish the first room you'll find it looking neater and might find yourself motivated to encourage all the occupants of the house to break their bad habits.

Let's explore a few some of the places to watch out for and ways to make the management of them better.

Garages, Patios, And Outside Storage

A big selling point on many homes is a great patio, extra-large garage, even that outside storage large enough for your riding lawnmower.

These spaces have their purpose and even things that belong in each. However, each is a magnet for collecting items that are soon forgotten. These forgotten things grow larger and larger until the space can no longer function as intended.

When you're ready to work on these spaces, put on some good music, layout the trash bags and some boxes then have someone help to keep you on track. In the garage or storage area, hang up tools or put them in their correct spots. Anything you haven't used in over a year should be assessed for usage value.

Yes, keep the water key needed to shut the water off in an emergency. No, don't keep that paint from three years ago. (Be sure to check with your local government on how to properly dispose of paint.)

If your yard tools are broken and you can't fix them, then it's time for them to go. If you can fix them, put the item aside and do that later. Don't interrupt cleaning to repair.

Look at the furniture and items on the patio carefully. Start with identifying furniture that is broken and unrepairable. Move that out of the way while you plan how to get rid of it. Find items on the patio that belong in other spaces and move them back to where they belong. Is this where you've piled the stuff to take to the donation center? Load it up and drop it off.

When you've finished putting these spaces back to normal make a plan to keep them up. It's very easy to put things down just anywhere and say you'll put them up later. It's better to take the extra few minutes to put them where they belong so you don't have to lose another day cleaning up again.

Now it's time to reward yourself. Get something to drink, crank up the music, and enjoy that patio again.

Boo! Attics And Basements

If you have an attic or basement that's not built out into a living space then these might be the dark scary places you hate to go. The problem with that is once items are put away in those spaces you have no desire to explore and organize the piles that build up over time. No one sees it so what's the problem?

It depends on your point of view. Do you want to find those holiday decorations and get them out? Maybe you put your off-season clothes there and it's time to rotate the closet. Either way, you have to go into the space and get past all the things you've shoved in there for later.

The first thing to do is to put some lighting in there. Even if it's temporary like a lamp on an extension cord, you need to see the entire space. And yes, music will keep the spooky feeling at bay, that is if you don't play themes from horror movies. Even better, take a friend to keep things light and moving.

Make a quick list of the categories of things stored there like decorations, clothes, broken down furniture, your childhood toys, or even all the things your ex-girlfriend gave you that you hated. Now decide how that space fits in your life. Is it destined to remain as storage or does it need to be finished out to become part of the house? If storage, what should be in there and what do you no longer need.

> **Caution:** Don't get throw away happy. It is good to keep a few things from your

> childhood to give to children, nieces, and nephews. Maybe it's time to share that with others now.

If the items in storage like decorations are no longer used, find them a new home. Donation centers, props for local performing arts centers, even crafters, might be interested in the stuff.

Off-season clothing is great as long as it wasn't off-season when you were twelve. Remember your closet cleaning lessons and apply them here. If you have five winter coats and now live in Florida, keep one that's versatile and in good shape. You might go to visit friends or travel for a meeting and need one. The rest need to find a new home.

Now that you're through cleaning and before you close the door make yourself a promise:

> "I promise not to put anything in the attic / basement that I won't use in the next twelve months OR that isn't held for the next generation."

Each time you open the door ask why you are putting the item in your hands in that room instead of keeping it in your main house to enjoy? Because out of sight equals low value.

Miscellaneous Closets

Hall closets, laundry room closets, even linen closets have a door and the "out of sight / out of mind" urge that goes with them. Think twice! These places have a purpose just like the bedroom and the kitchen. We've all seen the cartoon where someone opens the closet door and mounds of stuff tumbles out covering the person and the floor with its contents.

Hall closets are provided to hang coats, collect hats, gloves, and umbrellas, even to store vacuum cleaners. If you live in an apartment this is vital space sometimes used to store holiday decorations or folding chairs. When mom shows up for a surprise visit, just know she will find a reason to open that door. Don't hide anything in that closet you don't want her to find.

Linen closets not only hold towels, sheets, and extra blankets but sometimes pull extra duty with cleaning supplies, toilet paper, even first aid support. And if you're blessed to have other extra closets, be sure you determine their purpose and the reason you put each thing in them. Without a purpose, closets run amuck with mounds of stuff and you'll soon end up with the pile of stuff on the floor like in the cartoons.

As my family grew and they occasionally "helped" put laundry away, I would eventually find things that I'd been looking for stuffed and wrinkled in the back corner of the linen closet. So about once a year when I found myself in an organizing mood, I'd open that door. It was time to pull out things, fold, organize and put everything back in an orderly fashion. Now the world was at peace again (at least in my mind) and I wouldn't be embarrassed if someone went to get a band-aid out.

Remember that in most homes closet space is limited and precious. Like all the other rooms in your house they have a purpose and if not thought about will quickly become a catch-all that will require you to spend time cleaning out. Just remember that the closet holds items you use occasionally and if you haven't needed something in there for more than a year or two then maybe you need to get rid of it. This allows you to use the space for something you do need to get to.

So, either put the needed items away correctly the first time or pick a day to straighten it up. It's your time and your choice.

Flat Surfaces Are Calling You

If it's flat it's fair game. Nope! There are days in my home where I'd like to take all the flat surfaces and turn them into curves. Deep down I know my son would just consider that a challenge to balance things on, so POOF! There goes that bright idea.

There are two ways to look at flat surfaces. They hold a lot of things so everything is in reach and sometimes easy to spot. As a bonus, if you cover them in stuff, the counter no longer has to be dusted because there isn't room for dust.

On the other side, if it's covered in stuff, you might not be able to find things that end up buried at the bottom of the pile, and it makes you look like you're a slob. When everything is put away and the surface is empty, dusting is just a quick swipe and you're done.

I prefer a magic wand for dusting but will choose the quick swipe over the clutter!

LADIES WEAR ALMOST ANYTHING

Now that you've moved out the house clothes you might find that your budget for clothes took a big hit. Additionally, now you have to buy holiday gifts for the family and you've never had to do that either. Don't panic. Let's dig into some tips on how to buy clothes so you don't waste money.

In prior pages we've delved into things that make you happy. Looking good is another thing that makes people happy but it can be a bit tricky to determine the specific items that provide the comfort and confidence that make each person happy. Let's delve into tips to help you navigate these tricky waters starting with the ladies.

Okay ladies, don't puff up and try to say the guy's clothes are more complicated than ours are because you know that isn't true. We have sizes like petite, women's, and the unnamed regular set. Then we throw in a choice of sizes ranging from 0 to 28W or larger. And to complicate that a bit more throw in petite small to 4XL and they have no idea where to start shopping.

Solids, patterns, or stripes, short lengths, too long, pencil or A-line skirts, pleats or not, we have our opinions just like they do. Throw in skinny jeans, comfort fit, boot cut, and relaxed fit and we're setting them up for failure. Our closets overflow with a variety of brands, colors, sizes, and styles that can send any guy running to the nearest gift card rack rather than risk buying something you'll hate or more horrifically, is too small or too large.

Admit it. Most women have various pieces of clothing kept for when our weight goes up or down, and most men will never figure out what size you wear. If you want it, then write it down, add the size, and tell them where to buy it so you'll get just what you want.

And remember, if they complement anything you wear just say thank you for noticing. This is a slightly dangerous thing for men to do so be sure they know it is appreciated.

Ladies Undies - Proceed With Caution

Don't try to buy bras or underwear for a woman. Our bras have two key sizes like 32A or 44EEE. We choose between underwire or not, front or back hooks, low scooping fronts or high coverage, even something called a sports bra. The tags in our bras quickly lose their readability, so don't rely on reading the label and know what to buy.

And our undies provide just as much variety as the guys. Hip-hugger, bikinis, thongs, or briefs; we love variety, color options, even sassy sayings. The good news is the size label is pretty easy to read as long as you get the same brand and style.

If you want to make a sexy gift purchase, get help from her best friend on the size or sneak a peek in the drawer. Watch those fabrics because cheap lace can be a bit itchy and sparkle fabrics or latex are sometimes only meant for short term wear. Keep the lady comfy and confident with good choices.

Looking Good In Dresses, Shirts, Or Pants

As I mentioned before your best bet is to let the woman tell you what to buy. If you really want to surprise her with something, enlist the aid of her best friend, daughter, or mom. They can go shopping with her and feed you the information on what she liked. But don't wait to buy it because some sizes disappear quickly from the racks. (Even for online shopping, sizes go quickly.)

For those who still want to venture forward, here are a few tips.
- Look at shirt lengths. Some want them to hit just below the waistline, others want the back length to cover their bottom.
- Skirts and dresses might be wider only at the bottom for a swirl around flair while others are roomy from the top to the bottom.
- Like men's pants, options include flat fronts or pleats, stretchy fabrics or tailored looks. Tread cautiously if you don't want to offend her.

Before you start shopping, take time to look at what she's wearing. If you like the way it looks and she seems confident, that is a good thing. Don't put her in that skimpy tight-fitting pair of jeans if she likes the baggy ones. That might start a fight.

THE WORLD OF MANLY CLOTHES

Men like to think they're clothes aren't complicated — funny! They have a variety of styles, patterns, colors, and fabrics and, like for women, are an important statement of their personality. And don't forget those special things they wear like vests, cummerbunds, and ties that add to the complexity.

Each man has a style and trying to get the suit guy into sweatpants, or the shorts guy into a tuxedo, can be as big a challenge as climbing a mountain. Their style makes them happy. If you plan to buy something for them you need to understand what makes them happy.

The good news is there seems to be fewer places to buy things for men, so it can be a bit easier to get the right items. Easier, that is, if you don't want to change them, because they normally shop in the same place and their brands are true to their style. And easier because men's styles don't change often.

Knowing what the options are for the various pieces will guide you on making the current selections. Some of you might even find there are items that pique your interest to wear. Don't forget, trying new things can be fun.

Hidden Comfort - Underwear

Let's start our men's wear discussion down under. Boxers, briefs, trunks, boxer / briefs, thongs, or bikinis, whatever your style, men have a variety of choices. No longer stuck with a choice between tighty-whities or loose-fitting boxers, the world has embraced men's choices giving them options in fit and fabrics, and giving their family gifting fun.

Think about boxers with hearts or trunks with flirty sayings, even superhero boxers, that proudly show up for Valentine's Day or Christmas. As long as you stick to their style choice, you can have a lot of fun with colors and sayings.

> **Tip**: Watch out for itchy fabrics or things that might need ironing especially if the guy doesn't own an iron. There are only a select few men who want to iron their clothes and paying someone to do it for you might not be in their budget.

Undershirts are designed to be worn under another shirt to absorb sweat. These days, not all men choose to wear them under other shirts. However, if they do, there are things to know. V-neck or round neck normally in white or the occasional grey, they shouldn't show through the other shirt.

Comfortable and easy to wash fabrics are the most important things to know here. But watch that preference for neck shapes or percentage of cotton. If the selection is truly an "under it" shirt then it has to feel good to the wearer.

If you're buying a shirt for the tee-shirt guy, then be sure the fabrics are comfortable, and the fit matches his style, that is, if you want them to ever make it out of the closet or drawer.

Sleeves, Collars, Buttons - Shirts

Men's dress shirts are sized in neck dimensions and arm lengths, with widths listed as tailored, classic, full fit, or even athletic fit. Big & Tall is another grouping requiring you to look in a separate section of the store to get the right fit. As in all clothing, there are a variety of fabrics, color choices, and styles. Clothing is as important to a man as it is to a woman. If you get it wrong, they won't wear it. (And there goes the happy life.)

If you want to buy a shirt for a guy, start by taking a peek in his closet. Assess his colors and try to stick within those parameters if you want to get something he'll wear. You'll also probably find the selection of dress shits narrowed to a few key brand names making it easier to get something that's well-received.

Knowing how tall they are will guide your sales assistant on which section you need to shop in. Does he like standard three-button shirts, golf shirts (special breathable fabrics), button up the front, casual, or dressy. Check for preferences on long sleeves versus short sleeves as well. This will help you pick the part of the store to shop in and the basic information needed to get started.

You also need a bit of information about sizes. Take a look at the labels. Long sleeve shirts will look something like 16 ½ x 33/34. The first number (16 ½) is the neck size. The second number (33/34) is the sleeve length. The brand labels will give you some direction in the fit, but when in doubt, pick a salesclerk in the store to show you options that are similar in size and shape.

Men's dress shirts have cuff options as well and you need to take a look. Do they have buttons, or do they need cuff links to close them? Cuff links require a small stitched hole in each cuff that the cuff link goes into. More formal men might have French cuffs at the ends of the sleeves. That means the cuff folds back on itself before securing, normally with a cuff link. This type of shirt is very much a preference, and for those choosing cuff links, it opens other gift options.

And men don't stop there with their fun. Let's talk collars. Buttons, no buttons, hidden buttons, tabs, eyelets, stitching or not, wing tips, even band style collars. There's even something called a collar tab or collar stick that keeps those corners and edges looking neat.

A collar tab / stick is a piece of plastic or wood that slips in a hidden pocket on the back of the front points on a collar to keep those edges laying straight. When in doubt, take pictures with your cell phone and show them to the person in the store. Take a breath. It's not all that bad. The shirt brand tags will guide you a bit and a peek at the collar will be a big help.

If they're into golf shirts, watch brands and sizes. XL is not the same fit between sport shirt brands. And a three-button shirt is not the same as a golf shirt. The difference is found in both the fit and the fabric. Check for those brand tags or images on the shirt chest to get the right ones.

Fabric, Legs, And Zippers - Men's Pants

Pants are very similar to men's shirts in that they have a couple of measurements. They use waist size and leg length for measurements. 34 x 36 means a 34" waist and a 36" inseam (inside of the leg) length instead of neck and arm. Fabrics fit the wear, like dressy or casual. Full cuts for the fuller body might have pleats to expand the fit or elastic inserts in the waistband. Some come with a cuff at the bottom, or you might need boot cut for that cowboy boot he likes to wear. (Hurrah for cowboy boots!)

Relaxed fit normally means the butt and sides have a fuller, roomier cut, but read the label to see if they added more space in other areas for that fuller man in your life. And if he's the hearty athletic type, stick close to what he normally buys to be sure those muscles won't pop the seams.

When picking out jeans for men, the selections are similar to a woman's choices. Relaxed fit, short or long lengths, straight leg or boot cut, but it has to be comfortable or they won't wear it. Pay attention to fabrics, too. Does he like the stiffer starched look of crisp new jeans or the softer prewashed style? And be sure to watch for holes in their favorite pair. You don't want to go out with friends and tell him to be comfortable if you don't want him to wear that pair because that's all he likes. Help your guy have options.

Shorts for men come in two categories: casual wear and sportswear. Casual can mean the comfy old pair with holes or nicer "poolside" ones for summer parties.

Sports styles vary on what is appropriate for the game. Some guys will only wear one type of shorts, so don't waste your money buying what you like unless they agree to try them out.

All in all, what they wear on the bottom is part of their look and men *do* care – especially when it comes to comfort. Get it right or the gift will end up in the back of the closet, lonely and unloved. (Help. Let me out. It's dark in here!)

Knotting It Up With Ties

Plain, patterned, extra-long for a tall man, clip-on or bowtie, skinny or wide, this accessory is the place that men flex their personality in a large group.

Look around a room filled with men in suits and you'll notice some consistency in their appearances. Similar cuts with only a few standing out in a different fabric. Many will even wear similar shirt colors and styles. However, unless they are politicians (they stick with the red or blue of their party most times), their ties will be the place they show their personality. Be sure to embrace the fun of picking a tie and shirt combination they will be proud to wear, but don't defer to your preferences.

A personal note of thanks to all the dads out there who've suffered through wearing that "not so your style" tie for the sake of the child who gave it to you. Back in sixth grade, we made ties for our fathers. I picked a polyester fabric (think back to the 1970s) with a royal blue background, large dots and swirls of yellow, white, and hot pink.

Near the end of his life, I asked (with a bit of embarrassment) why my dad ever wore that horrible tie. His answer was simple. *You made it.* But I pressed on. What did others think of you? With a loving smile, his response was simple. *It was a gift my daughter made for me.* Other men completely understood the proud feeling he had and understood the reason for the tie. The tie said I loved him. Gotta love a man who will do that. Thank you, dad!

And before you guys get too proud about this little accessory, let's be clear on something. Ladies can wear ties. We find this fun fashion a playful addition to our wardrobe allowing us to throw off others making a sudden change in our look. Clip one on a dress shirt or knot it proudly allowing its design to bring a bit of color to that plain shirt. If you choose to wear a tie, do it proudly and have some fun. And hats off to all those dads who love us enough to wear whatever we make for you!

Cummerbunds And Suspenders

Cummerbunds are considered a formal accessory usually of pleated material and worn with a formal single-breasted dinner jacket. Ladies, it is not designed just to cover a man's belly. It is always worn with a bow tie because it would get tangled up in a regular tie. Cumber Buns come in a variety of colors and patterns.

This is another instance where a man can show his personality, even matching the fabric to the tie. I've seen colors to match a bride's maid's dress, camouflage for the senior prom guy, even paisley prints. Many times, these will be coordinated with a bow tie to *tie up* the connection. (Forgive the pun.)

Like cummerbunds, suspenders offer style options and not just a way to keep your pants up. Some have clips and others need buttons to connect them to pants. Colors or patterns for the elastic and hardware finishes can make this a dressy or just plain fun accessory. Belts leave that bit of a belly hanging over the top. Suspenders keep the pants covering the tummy without drawing attention to your love of food.

Adding suspenders to a suit can change the impression others have of you when it's time to take off the jacket and roll up the sleeves. Gentlemen, this is your opportunity to express yourself so go for it.

Vests - Not Just For Freezing Temps

This versatile item has two distinctly different reasons to come out of the closet. Winter winds will whip through a shirt but a vest provides a barrier to keep your manly body warm and snuggly. The second reason is for those formal wear occasions where you need to step up to a very dressy look.

A vest provides the opportunity to make a statement with a variety of colors and fabrics. Solid colors, camo, even plaid, some guys take the opportunity to be sure everyone is looking at them, assessing the statement they are making with their selection. This additional layer isn't for everyone as it does provide insulation. That hot-natured guy isn't a candidate for the stylish Scottish plaid vest you found on sale.

However, the outdoors guy might enjoy the padded outdoor winter vest in a cool looking fabric. If he's a hunter, find that camo print to match his preferred hunting time. If he has a bit of a belly, he'll need a roomy cut around the middle. Don't forget to watch the fit.

STORING YOUR WEARABLES

Since running around naked isn't socially acceptable in most places, you need clothes. But clothes seem to multiply like rabbits. There are days I think clothes are really an alien life form because they grow legs and move to other rooms to live, making it look like the laundry hamper threw up. That's right, they move, because surely you wouldn't leave them lying around where you had to go back and find them to wash or even re-wear that favorite pair of faded blue jeans.

Of course, some of the college guys I've known want to smell that shirt from the floor and possibly wear it for the second or even third time before washing. Let's just hope they grew out of that habit when they graduated. Yes, wearing something several times saves on water, laundry detergent, and time. However, that "less than fresh" smell might cost you the attention of the very person you like or even your job.

Let's explore clothes and their storage as a life process.

Hangers, Rods, Shelves - The Closet

This is considered a part of the bedroom and a place to put in an hour or so cleaning and organizing. Don't start this challenge without a friend. A really good friend. The friend's job is to be honest by challenging you to let go of things you don't wear or that don't look good on you anymore. Yes, you can keep one outfit from the '80s to wear to a costume party, but only one! This goes for any ten-year cycle of clothing - only one vintage outfit for parties, letting the rest go to a new home. After all, if you don't wear something, it gets lonely hiding out in that dark closet.

There is an old rule that if you haven't worn it in two years, part with it. This is where the friend is supposed to help you pare things down, opening up your closet space for new opportunities. It does not mean go out shopping to replace them! If you have enough clothes to go without washing for a month, then you probably have too many.

I know this sounds harsh, but let's put it in perspective. Large amounts of clothes take a lot of time and money. You need to wash and put away the clothes and the increasing number of items requires more storage space, hangers, or organizational containers. The more time you have to spend on clothing care the less time, and maybe money, there is for play. Balance is essential to easy living.

The clothes remaining in the keep pile after your purge will need a bit of attention. Start by sorting them into groups by what you wear. Groups like shirts, pants, dresses, skirts, suits, and sweaters. Casual, day job, getting dirty, dressing up, even special occasions might fit your way of sorting a bit better.

Look at the closet and decide what you should hang up and what to fold for placement on a shelf or in a drawer. Stacking neatly folded jeans, sweaters, shorts, or even tee-shirts takes less space leaving the hanging section for the more appropriate items or those that wrinkle. Don't forget to find a place for swimwear, nightgowns, robes, underwear, and socks.

Then there are all those accessories like skullcaps / do-rags, ties, belts, scarves, muscle shirts, jackets, and more. Here are a few quick ideas for these miscellaneous items, but let your imagination go with ideas and solutions to fit your lifestyle.

- Tie hangers come in all types of options but their use isn't limited to ties. Use them for belts, ties, do-rags, scarves, jewelry, and more.
  o I bought the board with zigzag pegs to hang on a back wall of the closet for my husband's do-rags and my longer necklaces. It's also very easy when putting away the laundry to quickly hang the do-rags on the pegs.
  o Cup hooks screwed into a board is another easy option. Mount it on the back wall of your closet behind the clothes. It worked great when the kids were little and could be placed at a height they could access. It held belts, ties, jewelry, and even a few toys that came on a loop or chain.

- o Tie hangers that work by hanging like a coat hanger can also work for things like scarves, belts, hair bows, and more.
- Baskets on the floor or shelves are great for folded scarves, rolled belts, seasonal gloves / hats, and slippers.
- Storage cubes come in plastic or wood and multiple sizes.
  - o Put a board through the middle and you have a rack with two rows for shoes.
  - o Configurations include stacking them or placing them on the floor or shelf for easy access.
  - o Roll up your leggings putting them in the cube instead of a drawer.
- Protect the shape of your boots. Use a few of those empty cardboard paper towel tubes to stuff in your boots. This will provide a bit of stiffness to help them hold their shape and the open centers allow air to flow to the bottom.

- Chain coat hangers. These hangers have an extra hook in the middle that can link several hangers together vertically giving you more horizontal space in the closet. This is a great way to compress storage for the off-season or special occasion clothes. You can even cover them with a plastic clothing bag or garbage bag to keep the dust off everything until the season comes around again.
- Over the door organizer pockets aren't just for shoes. Umbrellas, scarves, jewelry, brushes, make up, and belts fit great in the pockets and keep things in an easy to access place.

Do you have young children? Be sure to put clothes in places they can reach. If you start letting them help select their outfits and put away laundry at a young age it is easier to build the habit with some fun making it less like a chore.

Pairing clothes into outfits makes picking something to wear not only easier for the child, but also for the parent with no sense of clothing coordination. This is as easy as hanging or folding shirts and pants / shorts together as you put them away.

Remember a minute or two of organizing things as they come out of the dryer means less work when you reach the bedroom. Use the tops of the machines to layout items until you match them. Then with a quick fold or hang, you're done.

Where Are My Clothes Hangers?

Do you grab a shirt leaving the hanger on the bar in the middle of the remaining shirts? Then when it's laundry time, you have to dig out the hangers. That is time-consuming and a bummer tied to a chore most of us hate… laundry.

Well with your newly cleaned closet, there is an easy solution. Pick a spot on the end of an easy to reach shelf, at the end of the hanging bar, or even place a basket on the floor just below your clothes, for the empty hangers.

Every time you take a piece of clothing off a hanger put it in this spot. Now when it's time to do laundry it's very easy to grab the hangers and stuff them in the top of the dirty clothes basket, then carry everything to the laundry room together.

When clothes come out of the dryer, hang them or fold them based on how you'll put them away. Have a small basket or plastic bin handy to help with sorting. I keep a small plastic tub for each person in the family with a color they like on a wire shelf over the washer / dryer for easy reach.

If you don't have a shelf, stack them nearby and place them on the laundry machine as you take a load out of the dryer. Fold underwear separating it from your matched socks and placing it in the correct bin. Now when you take these things to the bedroom you can put it all away in a matter of minutes because you did the sorting as you took it out of the dryer.

It's easy to give younger children their bin letting them help carry and put away. Since I generally have two to four loads of laundry per week, I put away each load as it comes out. This keeps the chore chopped into small bites and doesn't feel overwhelming like waiting until all of the clothes are clean and dry.

> **Tip:** If you wait for two or more weeks to do laundry, this easy task will feel like a chore. Frequency makes it easier to complete.

Organizing Jewelry

If you have several necklaces and leave them in a pile, they are guaranteed to weave themselves into a giant knot. Earrings, pins, cufflinks, and tie clasps will jump into the knot and POOF! You can't wear or find your favorite pieces.

I saw this tip somewhere on social media. Buy a package of assorted sized buttons from the craft store. Each button will hold one pair. Push your earrings through the holes securing them with the backers on the other side.

If you wear the clip-on style, just use the larger buttons and clip on the pair. Worried about stretching the clip-on? Cut some felt into small one-inch squares. Then clip away. Now you don't weaken the clasp joint but your earrings are still easy to find.

You can place a pair of earrings on each button / square and into a drawer. This makes it easy to find and sort earrings if needed. Presto no more trying to find matching sets. These ideas will also work for men's cuff links or your favorite pin sets. Visit your local craft store to purchase packages of spare earring backers. Keep these along with those extra buttons or felt squares in a small box in a nearby drawer.

> **TIP:** See instructions on how to make your own box in the back of this book. Craft papers make this really fun.

Storing Your Wearables | 79

Now when you buy new earrings you can easily grab a button to put them on. And when you take the earrings off or on and feel that backer getting too lose, throw it away and grab another. I lost several favorite earrings when they fell out of my ear all because the backers wore out. Now the spares keep me from losing my favorite pieces of ear bling.

Do you have a collection of rings you enjoy wearing but they end up buried under other stuff? There are a couple of ideas on how to organize these. Buy a small square of Styrofoam and some toothpicks. Put the toothpicks in the block and slip the rings over them. Now they stay in place when you set them in the drawer. Another option is to place them in small craft organizer boxes that have partitioned sections. Snap the lid closed and slip into a drawer.

Those ponytail holders can be stored in a small plastic container, looped on an empty toilet paper roll, or slipped onto the hooks on a tie rack. If you have a hair ribbon collection, buy about three feet of wide ribbon and a plastic loop. Stitch one end of the ribbon over the loop and hang from a command strip or nail. Now clip those bows down the ribbon for easy access.

To keep the knots out of bracelets and necklaces, don't lay them in a drawer. Hanging them on a necklace rack or even cup hooks on the wall saves time taking out knots. You can also use this as a way to sort your jewelry using categories like work, play, or formal wear.

Get creative as you look for ways to store jewelry. Craft boxes with divided squares keep things separated. I found a piece of wall art at my local hobby

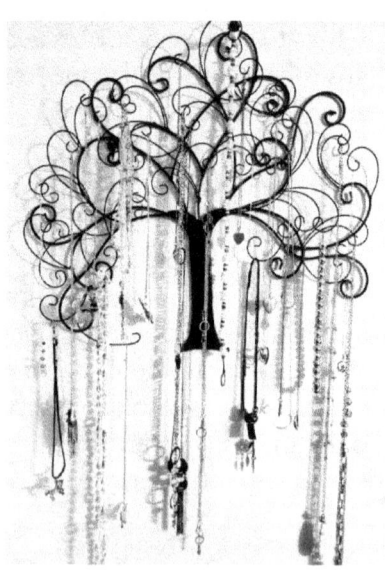

store and the metal curls were a great way to hold my necklaces. Now it's easy to find something and looks neat on the wall. I think it looks like a willow tree.

Buying Clothes

Casual, business, work, and after five all mean you need something specific to wear that matches the event. If you don't have the right thing in your closet, then you have to go shopping.

Shopping for clothes brings out a multitude of emotions in people. Some find it therapeutic. Others equate it to a toothache. I've heard people say their hobby is shopping and others just wait for Christmas and hope they receive something they can wear so they don't have to go clothes shopping.

Remembering what all the clothing terms mean when you start a new job or get an invitation to an event can cause a panic attack. You just need a bit of information to ease the panicky feeling and put you in the driver's seat. There are some quirky things about clothes that might also help you look at that next purchase a bit differently.

Did you know women's shirts button on the left and men's shirts button on the right? Historical sources say it goes back to the early days of buttons. An expensive item, when found on lady's clothing, it meant the person had wealth and wealthy ladies had maids to help them dress. The left side placement on a woman's garment made it easier for the person to help them to dress. But there's more to the differences than just where's the button. Sizing, names of the accessories, even types of fabric are different and very important.

This section is partly a guide on picking what to wear and partly a buying guide that can help with gifts for family, friends, or that special person in your life. Or maybe, it will help you understand some of the clothing puzzles in your life.

If you're shopping for yourself, you know about sizes, but you might want to check out some new styles to find a fresh look. Before you start shopping for someone else, you need to learn a bit about the person you're buying for because you want your gift to be enjoyed. Look at their color and style choices for work and play. Decide which category you want to buy for - work or play. If you're buying for a person who likes to wear all black or solids, don't buy them a florescent flower-patterned item, unless of course, it is a gag gift or for a theme party.

Don't let this overwhelm you. With some basic information on terms and sizes, you'll feel confident about your shopping missions and event wardrobes.

What To Wear

In today's world, you need a clothing clue about any event you're planning to attend or a new work environment. Evening events, weddings, or parties are about the taste of the person planning it and not about what is traditional. You need to know how to dress so you don't rush out to buy an expensive new item only to find everyone wearing blue jeans.

People bandy about terms like casual, business, business casual, come as you are, after five, cocktail, semi-formal, and formal. Work guidelines generally spell out things like "business" if suits are required. Business casual means no jeans but you don't have to wear a suit, tie or skirt.

If the job allows jeans, it normally specifies that your favorite ripped jeans are not acceptable. Read the guidelines and dress appropriately. Being underdressed for work can be the deciding factor on that promotion you've been trying for.

Parties normally give you information on what to wear on the invitation. If in doubt, either ask someone who has been there before or call the hostess for suggestions. Just remember if it is a co-ed or family party, be sure you control the amount of skin shown. It doesn't matter if you're a guy or a girl, those shorts with a bit of your butt cheek showing doesn't all ways look attractive. Save them for hanging out at home.

For pool parties, take along a cover-up or shirt for hanging out after the water. It's just polite. Besides, you might get chilly if the party moves inside to the air conditioning at some point.

Weddings are the worst at helping you know how to dress. Those closest to the wedding know it's going to be outside in the sun on a sweltering southern day in July or inside a very formal church or venue. That's an important tidbit that many times isn't on the wedding invitation. For those not in the bridal party, they might not get the information.

As the person putting on the wedding, please be nice to your guests. If you don't disclose the dress code on the invitation, then find a way to let them know. How would you feel about showing up in your favorite outfit and high heels only to find out you have to walk through a farm pasture to sit in the sun for an hour or more? Or maybe the guest loves to wear jeans and you forgot to tell them everyone would be wearing suits, dresses, or formal wear. You invite people to a wedding because they are important to the bride, groom, and their families. Treat your guests like you care that they are coming.

After five means a bit dressy for the ladies and suits for men, but not full-length sparkly dresses or tuxedos. Break out those items for formal events. If you're invited someplace like the governor's mansion or the White House, just ask their teams for advice. You'll probably need information on parking, arrival, and security anyway, so add it to the conversation. Believe me, they're used to it.

Going out to live theater these days offers a range of clothing options from after five to business casual. If you're going with a group, agree on the tone for the evening and enjoy it. Maybe even step out of your box and make it a dress-up occasion if you don't normally do that. Make it an evening to remember.

Keep in mind that you never know who'll you meet when you're out and about and you can't take back a first impression. Leave people thinking you care about your looks. It could land you a new job or a new significant other.

TRANSPORTATION

Cars, bicycles, ride-sharing, and buses are only a few of the ways people get around. Some cities and lifestyles rely on forms of transportation that you don't own or have to maintain, others need a car, motorcycle, or scooter to get to work or to the store. If you're into ride-sharing car services like Uber and Lyft, the subway, or even taxicabs, I recommend you add that to your budget requirements we covered in the first Adulting Doesn't Have to Suck! book. Be sure to research any applicable guidelines for tipping as those things change.

For those into the personal vehicle lifestyle, there's a lot to picking out something that fits your needs, wants, and budgets. The selected vehicle will need caring for, protection from damage, and a general understanding of how it works. Let's explore some of this together.

Emergency Preparedness

Always being prepared for the stuff life throws at you means a little pre-planning by keeping a few things in the car. Umbrellas (2), a sweater, a small towel, paper/pen, cell phone charger, even sunglasses can provide a quick fix to keep you on the road to happiness. If you use public transportation consider a small backpack that holds some of them along with your purse if you have one. Then you're ready for anything.

Additionally, emergencies can be different based on the part of the country where you live. There are a few items you should consider keeping in your car and they can vary by the time of year. A blanket for colder areas, a roadside reflector to warn people if you are broken down, jumper cables, even a flashlight comes in handy. I recommend some of the new flashlights that you wind up so you don't have to worry about batteries.

If you travel in a lot of remote areas, you might look into the canned tire repair and the type of car starter that doesn't require another vehicle to make it work. I also have an ice scraper with a brush for snow and ice removal, and reflective windshield screens I can put up to keep out the hot summer sun.

Here are a few other tips to jump-start your thinking.
- A towel is a wonderful thing with multiple uses. It's handy to clean up spills, help with a car sick person, warm-up someone who's cold, cover a seat to protect it from wet or dirty

people or animals, clean windows or your glasses, and many more things.
- A small fire extinguisher comes in handy in case of car fires in wrecks.
- A small first aid kit with band-aids, scissors and tape have many uses.
- For those of us in sales a brush, makeup, paper and pin for un-planned sales calls, tissues, and loose change for tollbooths are also helpful.
- Keep a sweater or extra tee shirt tucked in the back storage area for clothing emergencies or just someone who is cold.

Your car emergency supplies are really about your life. When my children were small, I always had a few small stuffed animals that were not allowed to leave the car. These were considered trusted travel friends and provided cheering up when growing up became a bit too much life for them.

Protecting your automotive investment with some basic steps will save you time and money. Always lock the car with the key fob, if you have one, to set the alarm or at the very least be sure all the doors are locked.

> **Tip:** DO NOT leave things in sight including money, compact discs, computers, books, shopping bags, etc. These are just too tempting for some people and they just can't help breaking your window and taking what they want.

Remind yourself that the deductible on your insurance will come out of your pocket before the insurance kicks in and unless you have an endless cash flow (doubtful), then I suggest you hide things in the trunk, under a seat, or under a cargo cover. You would rather spend that deductible on fun than on a window and don't forget the time you will lose from work filing a police report and getting the window repaired.

Car Tips

Protect your license plates with some simple plate covers that will keep people from cutting off your renewal stickers or taking the entire plate. Some people like that you spend your money on renewals and then let them use the products. Then you win the lottery and get to pay even more money to get a replacement and you might get a bonus prize if the police pull you over for the missing items and give you a ticket.

If gas prices are starting to rise, you might look into a locking gas cap to keep people from stealing gas from you. Newer cars might not have that option but the thief does have to use a special device to keep the tank opening from closing down the siphon tube.

Some cars have expensive hubcaps. Check with your local automotive parts store and see if there is a way to lock them onto the car to protect them.

Keep in mind you can put locks and security systems on your car, but you won't be able to fully protect it if someone really wants to steal it or break into it. So always be aware of where you park your car. Is there security? Is it a high crime area? Keep your keys close to you and be aware of your surroundings. Some people will just wait for you to open the car and then attack you to get the vehicle. Others will watch you, steal the keys you casually laid on the counter and now the car is in their control. Plus, if you have any information in the car about where you live, like the required registration, they now have your home keys as well.

There are several companies that offer some great accessories for SUVs and cars. I love the plastic "bed liner" mat that my husband bought for my SUV. The removable matt has a small lip that catches the spilled bottle of milk that tips over while driving, captures the dirt from the plants I buy, and keeps wet stuff from getting the carpet yucky.

Vent visors are another great option. These little plastic strips adhere to the car doors over the windows. Now you can crack the windows on rainy days to balance the moisture in the car or vent your locked car in the parking lot.

Turn Signals - Are They Optional Features?

Driving around town every day, it's fun to look at all the differences in the vehicles people drive and how they drive them. Deliberately safe drivers move through traffic gripping the wheel while the organ donor driver whizzes past them weaving in and out of traffic.

The standard features on a car are the only thing these two types of drivers have in common. Locks, doors, tires, windshield wipers, lights, and turn signals are standards, except on race cars. However, owners see some of these features as optional instead of a must-have worth every penny.

Would you drive around without tires? I see you rolling those eyes at my idea. Rims would rut the road and make it a very rough ride without that layer of rubber around them. How about no working lights? With city lights and other drivers lighting the way, you might think it wouldn't be a big deal. In addition to risking attention from the local police, you'd find other drivers flashing lights at you trying to keep you safe.

What I don't understand is why using the standard feature of a turn signal seems optional to some drivers. Being certain others know which direction you plan to go puts them on notice to either avoid you or alert you to danger. In turn, this protects both vehicles and makes the standard signal feature one that should be on the list of the most desirable features to have. (Wrecks cost money. Just saying.)

Heck, when you were a kid didn't you enjoy flipping switches and making lights flash? Growing up means you get to play with buttons, knobs, and levers without anyone telling you not to touch. Your car provides a variety of cool things that should excite your inner childlike making wipers move, windows go up and down, and lights flash.

Next time you're driving through town, take a moment to consider the value found in the many features of your vehicle. Enjoy getting to flip on that tick, tick, tick, making lights flash to alert others to the fact you have somewhere to be and plan on arriving, even putting the window up and down, letting you take in or avoid the outside air. Let your inner child have a little fun!

WORKING SMARTER

It's time to explore what you like about your work life. Pull out that trusty paper and pen again and get into a comfy chair. Think about what you do for a living, your work environment, and what that says about your likes and dislikes. Do you enjoy working alone or in groups? Some people love meetings and delegating work to others where others get the shakes just thinking of a meeting. Are you a stacker or a filer? Do you prefer to work from sticky notes or lists? Which traits of your co-workers do you admire and which make you crazy?

Just like you learned about your personal life, you need to spend time learning your likes and dislikes about the way you make money. Find out how you feel about working with others, do you want to be behind a desk or driving farm equipment, maybe it's that you prefer to work all night and sleep all day. This information will give you the basics needed to analyze your work life and where you might want to make a few changes.

Not only will this make your life easier, but you might get the attention of others. It could even help you get that next promotion. Look at how the people around you do their jobs assessing what impresses you and what makes you crazy.

The next step is a bit brutal. It's time to assess what type of image you're presenting to others. Do you interrupt or talk over others? Maybe you never voice your opinion on a conference call even if you know something is wrong. If your desk is always so covered in papers you can't find a flat surface to write on, how do you think others interpret that? Do others struggle to read your reports because of sloppy handwriting or maybe your paperwork is a crumpled mess buried somewhere in your truck instead of filed in its proper place.

For those really gutsy people, you can ask a co-worker to sit down with you and get some feedback on the way people see you. (Be sure to thank them!) Now challenge yourself to make some changes and step your work life up a notch.

Don't limit your thinking to office workers as the only people who need to have good habits and show others, they're smart about their jobs. Mechanics need a way to keep up with their tools. Some of them are very expensive and leaving one behind at a worksite can add up quickly. How mechanics clean and store their tools demonstrates the level of detail they use on the job.

Truck drivers need to keep up with maintenance on their vehicle, law changes that impact their work, even paperwork needed to pick up, deliver, and get paid for the job. Maybe you drive trucks but also maintain a CPR certification, have trained on how to handle an emergency spill of the product you're hauling, or have completed special training on how to make minor repairs to the vehicle. These extras demonstrate a desire to be good at the job under any situation. It says, *I am the employee you need.*

Construction teams have to keep up with occupational safety law changes, tools to do their job, even certifications showing they know how to correctly use that special big rig crane or other equipment. Some of these positions require you to understand how to read special things like site plans or work with minimal supervision. Be sure you know how to articulate those skills and can show that you know when to call a manager for assistance.

Nurses, emergency responders, teachers, restaurant workers, even trash collectors all have information about how to do their jobs as it changes. Getting that great review from the boss is about showing them you are keeping up with the paperwork needed by the company, you've applied the information learned from that last training session, and you've treated your job and those around you with a positive professional attitude.

Being positive, eager to learn, flexible, and open-minded takes you from "just getting paid" to "employee we want to keep" status. If you see a new way to do something that will make things better, share the idea with your boss. Some of the best process changes come from the person actually doing the work. Working smarter is always better than working harder.

> **Tip:** Going to a training class or meeting? Take paper and pen so you can take notes. It helps you stay awake during a boring presentation and says you take the meeting seriously.

Ask a friend in the hiring industry or in a manager role to help you review your resume. You can better track your career goals and identify your weak points if you know what others are looking for. If you plan on competing for another position research the same or similar job in other companies. Look for ones that are hiring and review their job descriptions. Knowing what skills are needed in that next job up the chain can help you determine what training you need to complete.

> **Tip:** Here's another meeting tactic. Have a separate smaller note sheet to write down random thoughts that have nothing to do with the actual meeting notes. Words spark thoughts and not always on topic. To stay focused, you need a place to put the other thoughts so your mind will allow you to return to the meeting.

Make a plan to learn something new. Pick out classes you should take to make you more productive like advanced Excel, PowerPoint, specialized computer or occupational certifications, a programming language, training for manufacturing equipment repair, management classes, safety improvements, or even project management.

As you implement the ideas from this chapter, I encourage you to start slowly. Pick 2 things you want to change and set a limit on how much time you'll spend making changes. Use the limited time surrounding your changes to get what you're seeking. This may mean not only changes in the way your office and emails are organized, but what you wear, how you speak and interact with others, or even who you eat lunch with. You spend a lot of time at work. Getting to know those you work with can make the time more enjoyable.

This short span of time allows you to make new impressions on people, become someone new, or step into something more than you are now. You will find this opportunity very few times without changing companies so be sure that as you lay out the plan to change your office, appearance, behavior, and email management that the pieces fit the new employee that you want to become.

Sit back and watch the people around you and see who takes notice. Those will be the people who get the big picture of how the office is an extension of themselves and how important it is to be happy at work. The others are so caught up in themselves and the job that they have become a working zombie. Maybe, just maybe, you might wake up and find you've been a zombie, too!

Ghosts Of Jobs Past - Business Cards

Keep a business card or contact record in your phone or email list for everywhere you have worked and one for your bosses. It is much easier to get in touch with people when you need to provide references. On the back of the card or in the file, notate the dates you worked there, pay levels, and your titles.

Don't forget that business cards are not just for your day job. If you have a family, make a business card for home. This was a very easy way to provide contact information to daycares, friends, teachers, etc., for my younger children. They could hand off the card and say call me or mom.

If you have a hobby, make a card that promotes your fun. Use it to connect with new suppliers for the raw materials or give to family to help them with ideas for gift giving to support your hobby. Just include a handwritten note on the back about the products you need and where to get them to make gift giving easy. And if you make stuff during your hobby time, use the card to help you sell the finished products. After all, hobbies are fun, but you don't have room to keep all the things you make.

Don't like paper cards? Word Docs or Excel Spreadsheets can be utilized to organize this information and stored with your resume for easy use.

The Office Appearance

So, you need to learn how to look organized, be productive, and make a difference in your company? And while doing this, you need to be sure others can see how you contribute to the company and to your co-worker's goals. To some, this sounds really easy, and it can be if you focus on it all the time. To others, this is just stupid because you don't care what others think and you're already too stressed out to care.

The reality is, you are probably very busy at work and don't have time to spend a week on a makeover. If you don't have much time, then you'll need to find small changes and implement them slowly so you have time to focus on getting the work done.

If your desk and floor are covered in piles of documents, or your email regularly stops working because it is out of space, you can easily spot some opportunities for change. Use this as an indicator that it's time to do a little re-organizing of those areas just like you did at home. Set a limit on how much time you'll spend on this so you don't overthink things. You can get lost in organizing and never get the job done.

I recommend limiting paper on a desk because it is one disaster away from disappearing. A tornado, hurricane, or fire could wipe out all your information… Poof! But if you're trusting your computer to store the data, be sure it's backed up off-site so there are options. Even laptops and desktops crash. Your work needs a protection plan.

Take time to look at what your desk and work area say about you. Does your desk have so many piles on the top, and surrounding it on the floor, that your co-workers are scared to give you anything for fear they will never get it back? Or maybe your desk is so empty that people are beginning to wonder if you really do any work? Organizing is as much about working effectively as it is about the impression you make on others.

Employees, managers, even vendors want to know they can trust you to help them quickly and efficiently so they can meet their deadlines. If you spend hours looking for simple information, they will look for some else to help them.

As you begin organizing, be sure to think about the types of information you regularly pull out for others and be sure to place it in an easy to access location. Now they get the impression you are easy to work with and feel confident that the information you provided is accurate.

Here are a few ideas to get you thinking.
- If you handle a couple of distinct different jobs and like paper files, pick a file folder color for each different category. Then organize within the color. If you like electronic files, then the top-level folders will be one for each job area with sub-folders organized by the time periods or sub-topics related to the work.

- Sticky notes come in a wide range of colors. Use these on file folders instead of writing on the folder tab. Not only do the colors allow you to color-code by projects or topics, but when

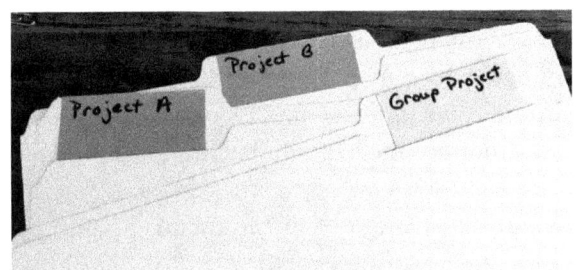

  the project is over, you can pop off the sticky and reuse the folder for your next project. (You did recycle all the paper in the files... Right!)

- Get a left-over paper box and stand all the folders up inside. Then organize and purge the completed projects. You can also use organizing racks from your office supply store to do the sorting by category. I keep an extra organizer under my desk for the times when work is busy and I have more to keep up with. Then during the slower times, I can remove the extra rack.
- Scan in the papers from completed projects and save them to your company file server. Then you have all the notes for future access and you can recycle the paper.

Is there another employee people always talk to? Find out why. They might have a lot of knowledge about the job and people find they are great about helping their co-workers. (Or they could just be friendly. It's good to be friendly, but don't let it keep you from getting the job done.)

If they are the "office brain" see if they have any organizing tips, especially those that utilize internal company resources. They might show you how to eliminate a duplicate process for someone in another department or stored data backup.

Remember, being organized means keeping your eyes open for new options. The world is changing and you have to make a few alterations if you want to keep up.

Emails Multiply Like Rabbits

Are there days where you wonder why your emails multiple like rabbits? My inbox is a mix of emails I've sent, new emails, responses from everyone on a project, even those pesky spam emails. If I don't stay on top of them, they multiply until I'm lost in a sea of words all screaming for my attention.

Organizing emails is easy with email folders and an archiving plan. Make folders to match the various projects you manage or by time period (week / month / quarter). If you are managing by topic or project, be sure to pull those off into an archive folder when the project is over.

The key to archiving emails is to schedule it regularly basis like monthly or quarterly. Be sure they are stored on a server that is backed up to protect you from hardware crashes, stolen computers, and that dastardly accidental delete. (Did you hear an evil snicker?)

Talk to others in your office and find out how they manage their emails. You'll find several methods and maybe even a few tips that might help you with your rabbits. Like your home, this is a chance to re-invent yourself.

As you begin making changes, you may find that your co-workers start to take notice and want to know what's up. Be happy that they noticed and always share your tips if asked. Being an office inspiration can be fun.

And remember, as your work role changes, you might need to adjust your email organizational style to fit with the new responsibilities. Using resources within your company to get information on how to make your job easier is also cost-effective. Ask your IT team for some tips on easy file management.

JOBS PAY THE BILLS

Wait, you don't have a job? Don't panic. Let's take a few steps back and get you set up to look for and land employment. Even if you have a job, I would read through this section just to help you think about things and be sure you are taking care of yourself and your income flow.

Have you always wanted to move up a level in the organization, get more recognition for the work you do, or get appointed to a specific committee? Maybe you want to move into another career. Like the changes in your home or work area, you have to plan what your goals are before you can achieve these changes. This goes for those who don't have a job currently. Maybe this is the time to go for that next step up, maybe you are ready to take a step back to reduce stress, or maybe it's time to completely change career paths while you seek a new job.

Start by investigating what skills you need to learn to make the change or get the next job. How many of the skills do you already have? Will it require you to get a special certification or degree? For the skills you're missing, look to see what classes are available online, in local learning companies, or community colleges. Checking out books from the library or buying books on the subjects you want to learn more about is another way to improve your knowledge base and it can even give you ideas on what direction you want to go. And free information is always a bonus.

How much will it cost to attain this change and how can you get some experience with these new skills while continuing to work in your current job or while you're unemployed? This could be another expense item in your budget plans, but one that could pay off with a better lifestyle in the long term.

Investigate if your company will help you pay for some of the costs if you agree to stay with the company for a specific amount of time or as part of hiring process for a new role. Some companies don't pay for anything and others only pay for classes or books if they relate to your current position. Your Human Resources department can provide more information on this topic.

When was the last time you had a career goals discussion with your boss? If he or she doesn't know you want to move up, they can't be of much help. Ask them for an assessment of your current knowledge and skills. Explain your new goals. Ask for suggestions on what you should learn, including technology and company infrastructure, and any other suggestions they have for reaching your goals.

If you think your current boss would hold you back and not be excited about your making these changes, you might want to skip them and either talk to someone in Human Resources or bounce ideas off some of your friends that you feel are very successful in their organizations.

Do some networking and look for people in other companies doing the type of work you are interested in moving into. These people can give you direction on things to learn, where to get knowledge and experience and may be able to help you get started in a new job in your area of interest. Offer to meet them for coffee or buy them lunch in exchange for a career exploration discussion.

Before you get too deep into looking for a new career or trying for that promotion, you need to brush up on a few key things. Let's talk about the basics of getting hired or promoted.

Start With A Resume

Do you have a resume? If not, you need to set one up. It doesn't matter if you are fifteen or fifty, you should have a resume. This is something you should start early and plan to spend a few minutes once a year updating. Keep them dated and save your old versions as this is great as a way to look back at what you've accomplished in your life. It can be a lot of fun.

Even if you've been in the same job for 20 years, keep this updated. You never know when your job could be eliminated, you have to move to another city, or you get a new boss you just can't stand and you want to begin looking for a new opportunity.

Yes, a fourteen-year-old can, and should, have a resume. This is a great way to get them to look at themselves the way other people would see them. It opens their eyes to a new part of life. It should include all the extra things they participate in like sports, scouts, clubs, church groups, even volunteering to clean up after a golf tournament so the team gets paid, should be on the resume.

Add things for special classes they've taken like babysitting, yoga, or maybe they are a member of a special mentoring program. Jobs can include almost anything they do such as yard cutting, picking up the mail for out of town neighbors, scoring or refereeing a sporting event, even helping with young children at church. Did they receive some special recognition in school for a project, won a writing contest or did they volunteer to be an officer for an organization? Maybe they performed in a play, worked building sets, helped with costumes, or did the marketing for the production.

As you grow older the resume should grow with you. At age thirty-five, you shouldn't include things from your teen years. but if you are a scout leader, coach or do volunteer work, these are just as important now as they were before. Companies like to hire well-rounded employees.

I'm guessing by now you adults have moved out of your parent's house and had a least one real job. You should add accomplishments from your employment history and be sure to include statistics showing how your work contributed to the company, where possible. Mention how you increased sales, saved specific dollars with a new contract, managed budgets, handled large dollars of payables or receivables, or some other dollar or percentage information. Mention specific projects and if you have changed positions within the company, be sure to make it clear what successes and skills you had in each job.

> **Caution:** Do not fudge the information on dollars or percentages, nor on what you did versus someone else on your team. Someone very knowledgeable on the topic will question how you achieved the results and might easily know if you are stretching the truth.

Also keep in mind that there are different kinds of resumes for different jobs, like electricians and mechanics, clerks, managers, supervisors, even upper-level executives. Look on the internet, talk to someone in human resources or even go to a professional resume writer to help you update yours before beginning any job hunt as formats and key information changes over time.

You will also need a second sheet that contains three to five people who are willing to be a reference for you. Of course, these should be people who think you are good at something. Some should be business references and one or two should be personal references. You want to pick people who come across as very professional, articulate, and of course, know you pretty well.

Ask each person in advance to be sure they are willing to be a reference for you. Then be sure they give you their first and last name, job title, and information on how they prefer to be contacted, like should the mailing address be home or work, phone number, or email. This sheet is only provided when requested by the company interviewing you and is usually done only if you are in the running for the position and not necessarily when you first apply.

Additionally, when you are ready to give the information to the potential employer, alert your references about the potential call giving them information on who might contact them and what type of work you are applying for. If the job requires special skills, alert them to things they know about you that are applicable to the new position. "Remember when I did X? This job uses that skill when doing Y process."

When it came time for me to leave the family business and try out a new career, my boss was my father. While I knew my dad would provide a glowing review of my skills, it might not impress a future employer. (I was his favorite kid after all… no, really. At least I wanted to think so.)

So, when writing my reference lists, I included my contact in a large company that was my customer. I spoke with him in advance and had his permission. My interview went great and the interviewer was impressed that I'd thought outside the box and asked one of my customers to be a reference. (Yes, I got the job.)

Practice Your Pitch

If you are starting to look for employment, find people you know and ask them to role-play interviewing with you to give you some practice. If they are managers or human resource professionals, that would give you the best help. Also, stand and look at yourself in a mirror and using a timer, practice a one-minute ad all about you. What is a one-minute ad? You have one minute to "sell" someone to hire you just like a one-minute commercial on TV or radio has one minute to "sell" a product or service.

What is the most important information other people should know about you? Your name, what type of work you do or are looking for, education and practical information that would influence people to want to look at your resume or talk to you. As you practice, you need to study your face. You should appear happy and confident, holding your head up. Do not fidget or bite your nails, slouch or play with your hair.

Here are a few ideas on elevator speech starters to get you thinking.
- Hello. My name is Pat Sawtelle. I'm writing a book about life tips and wondered if you had a great tip I could add to my book.
- Hi. I enjoyed hearing your thoughts about getting a job in engineering on the panel today. I'm looking for a position as an electrical engineer. Do you have any advice to help me in my search?
- I noticed you work for XYZ company. I just graduated from college (or high school) and am

interested in working for them. Do you have any tips on opportunities for someone with business analyst education?

Before the interview, look up information on the company. Be familiar with how the open position fits into the organization. Take a list of key questions to ask and be sure you get the answers. These questions should relate more to skills and work styles and not be only about pay, hours, and benefits. You want to appear interested in contributing and not just like you are there for a future paycheck.

If you're applying for a promotion, be sure to point out things you know about the company and how you can leverage that in the new role.

Being prepared and confident is important. If the interviewer asks a question you're not prepared for, stop and breathe. Don't rush to answer. Think about how that question relates to the job and if unsure, ask a return question to clarify the information needed.

The difference in you and the next candidate might be the questions you ask. Be prepared.

Dress For It

Look at your clothes. Be sure to pick outfits that present you as a professional and make you feel confident. This means being sure you don't have holes in the pants, your clothes are neat and fit well, and don't wear extra jewelry like a nose ring, eyebrow ring, or lip ring. If the job is in a conservative office, then no pink or blue in the hair. However, if fun hair colors fit with the culture of the company or you aren't sure, then ask about the dress code prior to the interview. Blue hair or nose rings might be a thing you get to add back after you start work there.

You will also need a very nice-looking folder to carry a few copies of your resume and reference sheets. You should also have a sheet of basic information that will be needed to complete the application forms and a few sheets you could write on to take notes during an interview. Application forms ask about dates and addresses where you have lived in the past; dates, company names, addresses and pay for past employment; dates, schools, and levels of education are other expected questions.

Now you're ready to get out there, land a job, and make some money.

BUSINESS SOFTWARE TIPS

Looking good at work comes in many forms. Of course, clothes, an organized office, and your attitude are important, but the emails, reports, and other information you provide give insight into the type of person you are.

Here are a few things to step up your game.
- For those with double monitors, you can make a print screen of the non-primary using the CTRL + ALT + Print Screen buttons together.
- Find the owner of a website you like. Enter *whois.net* into your search bar. Enter the URL for the website you want to learn about in the search box.
- Pivot Table Tips. Be sure the core lookup data is formatted the same way in both tables. Be sure all columns have a header. To insert a Pivot Table into a PowerPoint, highlight the data and use the CTRL C (copy) and CTRL V (paste) commands.
- Documenting processes are important for training new employees or remembering seldom used steps. Word allows both written information and inserted screenshots to build an easy to understand

document. It is also easy to update when they change.
- Date your documents. Dating a document (ex: Chalice Moon 12.31.13) provides a bit of interruption protection. Ever hit the delete button by accident? A plan to save versions over time in a backup folder means you don't lose everything with that mis-click. If you're sitting down to make major changes, the first step is saving a backup copy. Now make the file with the current date the one you want to change.
- When you need to solve a process problem be sure you understand the computer logic before making any changes. You can get from one to ten in several ways. Counting by one is easy, but if you count by twos you jump over some numbers. The skipped numbers could cause another process to break.
- Check your work. Double-check numbers, run spell-check and read the document out loud. All these steps will help you catch mistakes so the finished product has a positive understandability rating with the recipient.

> **Tip:** Spell check is not perfect. If your selected document review software tells you there is an error, be sure you agree. If not, check the error in another source. The English language is very tricky and computer checkers are not perfect.

Emails - Yep They Matter

Be sure you set up your emails to reflect a professional appearance. Take a few minutes to select a clean easy to read font and size. Putting your emails in Comic Sans or Dingbats while fun, might not get the type of attention you want. Arial or Helvetica are great fonts and if you just have to use one with serifs Times New Roman is a classic.

> **Trivia Tip:** Serifs are those little tails or pen strokes that hang off the letters in Times New Roman. Sans serifs essentially means without the extra pin strokes. Arial is a good example font for sans serifs.

Don't add extra graphics, color backgrounds, and other unnecessary things that make your email files larger or make them look like they have attachments. Those are not appreciated and many times may get your important message stuck in spam blockers.

Remember that emails are longer and more formal than a text message (no LOL, ROFL), but they are not a short story or novel! Get to the point. Use short sentences, bullet points, and even a few bold words to pull the reader through the copy.

If you want to get something accomplished be sure to ask for it. If you need a decision made write it so the recipient can answer with a simple yes or no. Clearly supporting an option, providing a recommendation, and asking for agreement makes it easy to get a response.

Subject lines are clues to the topic and help with searches later. Don't be tempted to "hijack" an email chain and change topics without changing the subject line. It can mess up your filing, searches, and effectiveness.

And for to love of Yoda, run spell checker and give it a last proofreading before sending it out.

Everyday Formulas

For those non-math types like me, we know what we want to understand but remembering the formula to put in Excel or the calculator is a pain. I might only need to use the formula once a year and my brain would rather remember where I put my keys or who I'm meeting for dinner more than a math formula.

Here are a few business use formulas that come in handy. Put a tab on this page or turn to the trusty (sometimes) internet and look for them on the fly.

- Looking for a value on a separate Excel sheet? To return a yes or no answer, use this one. =IF(CountIf(range_of_data_to_search,value_to_look_for), "YES", "NO")
    - Build the "Count IF" part then add the parts outside of that ( ) section.
- To get rid of division by zero errors - add this error code to the base formula to point out concerns. IF(ISError(formula),0,formula)
- Calculating Markup - Budgeting a total spend of $10,000 and 47% markup? 10000/1.47 = working $6802.72; 10000-6802.72 = fee of $3,197.28
- Calculating Margin on $10,000- For a 25% margin 25/75 = .3333, 10000*.3333 = $3,333. For a 40% margin 40/60 = .6667, 10000*.6667 = $6,667.
- Year over Year change percentage - Let's look at the change between 2019 and 2018 using the

last two digits of the year for the formula. 19-18 / 18 = % change.
- Cost as a percentage of revenue. Cost / revenue = %.

When working with formulas, be sure to format the answer so you get a percent instead of dollars if that is what you want.

Ask The Experts

If you need to complete a task in Excel, Word, PowerPoint, Adobe products, or even some other special software your company uses, and you don't know how to do it, you have a couple of choices.

For the more common programs, and even a few not so common, you can do a quick Google / Bing / Safari search (pick your favorite) on the topic. Many times, you'll quickly find great instructions ready to help you. Be sure to watch out for differences by software version, or check the date on the post is somewhat recent. If the post is five years old on a Microsoft or Windows question, it might be out of date for your software version and not greatly helpful.

If you are totally terrified to do an online search (gasp!) or the program is specialized and no information is found, turn to others in the office. Being willing to ask those around you how to accomplish something, shows you value their knowledge and that you care about the information you are working on.

Just remember if someone asks you how to do something (maybe more than once) that you graciously share the information they need. When you're comfortable with a topic, you sometimes spill it out too quickly for the recipient. They might need a few lessons to get a full understanding of the information.

LIFE PLANS

Have you've been complaining about life getting harder as you got older? Yes, looking back kindergarten seemed like the perfect place, but even it had challenges. Adults were always telling you things like *be nice*, *go to bed*, *be quiet*, even *put your toys away*. At five you were finally in big kid school and thought you knew it all. We're getting closer to the end of this round of advice and some of the remaining topics are silly while others just fall into the world is changing category. Hang in there. You Can Do This!

The first thing to know about life plans is that they change. You should have a goal and plans on how to get there but be willing to make changes. New people you meet, changes in technology, even job changes open you to decisions you hadn't planned for. Each of these can shift your plans. The key to a life plan is being open to altering them as life gives you new opportunities.

Ugh! Insurance

This is a topic everyone hates until the day they need it. I am not going to delve deep into these matters because they change constantly. Here are a few tips to guide you in your research and decision-making process.

- **Health Insurance.** When you are healthy, this seems like an expense to skip, but it's not. Federal laws change yet they can penalize you for not having health insurance. Additionally, the first time you have to go to the hospital emergency room and you have a $3,000 bill, you'll be upset.

    First, because with insurance you might only have to fork over a co-pay like $250. Secondly, because insurance companies make deals so they get deep (like 30% or higher) discounts on the bill where someone with no insurance might pay 100%. Yes, you can talk to the provider about getting discounts and setting up a payment plan, but who wants to do all that work?

- **Life Insurance.** Whole life, term life, universal life, level term life all these things just confuse me. Remember - Life insurance is not for your use. It is for those you leave behind to pay the bills you left and possibly make their lives a bit better.

If you don't have much money then use a savings account or investment account so you can still reach the money in an emergency. And definitely begin putting money into retirement before buying life insurance.

When you are ready to buy ask family and friends you trust questions about what they bought and why then get lots of referrals to help you find a good agent.

Retirement Accounts

Just get started. Today is never too late! You don't know how long you'll live. Think about that budget you set up earlier. That's how much money you need to live on if you were at retirement age today. Social Security varies based on the age you retire but you might only receive about 45% of what you earn today. How would you live off that? Zap! Probably not the way you want to live.

The government outlines retirement savings sometimes limiting how much you can put each year into certain types of accounts. Ask your employer or tax person to help you get things set up.

For those in private industry, your employer might offer to match a percentage of the money you put in your company retirement account each year. That's FREE money so put some in your account and say yes to the match.
- Put $1000 in the account during the year and they match 4%. 1000x.04=$40 FREE.
- Now do that every year for 40 years. 40*40=$1,600 in money they gave you! And that's before the interest things earn.

Keep in mind that the cost of everything goes up each year so you need to plan for it. You also need money for those medical bills that accompany aging. If you plan well you might have enough left over for fun like travel or family vacations.

My New Year's Resolution Is Turning To Dust

It's mid-January and like a vampire when you stake them, many New Year's Resolutions are already turning to dust. We start the year filled with hopes and dreams of what this new beginning holds like the exciting promise of spring on a cold winter day.

However, we tend to make proclamations for things to accomplish that take a little more effort than we imagined when the clock struck midnight. By this time of the first month, we've found multiple excuses that keep us from reaching our goal.

Today I challenge you to take a baby step toward your goal or adjust it to something a bit more attainable. If you promised to start exercising, start with five minutes a day instead of thirty. Do it while you watch your favorite TV show. If you wanted to learn to cook, plan a week's worth of simple meals using that new Instant Pot you won at the holiday party.

Some of you have decided that your planned resolution was a bad idea. Don't let the resolution dust create more work explaining why it didn't fit your life. Set a new goal! I recommend exploring the world of books maybe even reading a new author or trying a new genre. Ask friends and family what they're reading. Explore the library or a small local bookstore. Visit Goodreads, Bookbub, your favorite bookstores, or publisher sites to explore reviews and book excerpts that will spark a new interest.

Whatever new resolution you choose to try, start with five minutes a day and let the good times pull you into a new part of life. If you get off track, then brush yourself off and start again. You didn't learn to ride a bike or drive a car the first time. Keep working at it and you'll get better.

Happy New Year to all, and to all a good book tonight!

END OF LIFE PLANNING

This is not a chapter anyone wants to read but *please* do. Having your affairs in order at any age is important to those you might leave behind. Sudden illnesses, a car wreck, acts of terrorism, house fires, drownings, and more fill the news stories about the untimely death of those young and old.

At that point, you don't care about things, but those close to you have to deal with the loss of your life, along with the end of life costs and plans. A few simple things can be set up to provide information on your wishes making their lives easier so they can focus on remembering your laughter and life.

Keeping your bills organized means it will be easier for them to close out your financial affairs. Having information on file with all your vendors and health care providers about key people who can talk about your accounts will make their job easier.

Be sure people close to you know if you want a big traditional funeral, special religious event, cremation, or that you want your body donated to science. Having these decisions made, and pre-funded if you can, will make it easier for them as they deal with missing you and saying good-bye.

> **Favor:** Consider organ donation. You could bring life to another person and years of joy to their family with the gift of something you no longer need. Mark the choice on your driver's license and tell your family.

Let's start by defining end of life. It is not the day you can no longer live in your own home nor is it the day you break up with your significant other. End of life is the moment that either you've been told you have a very short time to live or the moment you are declared dead.

Let's dive into some easy to do steps that you can easily take care of then tuck away and not think of again. The most difficult step is finding a person you trust with this information.

Wills Or A Power Of Attorney

Having a Last Will and Testament, a Power of Attorney and written instructions on how you want to run your life or how to handle your body if you die are not things people like to think about. No one wants to think they'll die until they are too old to care what happens to their few remaining assets, but things happen. If in doubt, watch the news for a week. Deaths from robberies, murders, car accidents, or even fires take the lives of people of all ages.

A Will is a document that says who will be in charge of closing out your final bills and distributing your remaining material possessions. Attorneys can pass the hours regaling you with stories of family fights about what dad intended for that sibling to do versus what the sibling really did after he died. Write that Will and set the family up to stay close. If you want that bedroom suite or favorite watch or ring to go to someone, spell it out.

A Power of Attorney (POA) gives someone the legal right to act for you in various matters as spelled out in the document. Generally, there are a couple of important POA types. The first is the ability to handle your affairs like bills, assets, talk to attorneys, or businesses where you owe money. You can set this for "only if I die" or you can add clauses to cover them acting on your behalf if certain conditions exist like you're going away for 6 months. Tell your attorney everything so it can be written correctly.

The second is one strictly for making decisions about your health if you are mentally or physically unable to make the decisions and is called a Medical Power of Attorney. This includes withholding life support like ventilators so get an attorney to explain it to you before selecting that person. If you are concerned about that really tough time, give the power to say two people but spell out how the decision is made if they don't agree. If you are really worried about their feelings, spend time making notes they can refer to on your preferences and don't make them rely on memories from a brief discussion twenty years before.

Worried that you don't have the money to pay for these legal documents? Check with your local legal aid to see if you qualify for free or reduced fees assistance. At the very least get some forms off the internet, document your desires, and be sure to get your signature notarized.

For The Military

Did you serve in the military? Gather your key DD214s and put a copy with your will. Talk to the VA (Veteran's Administration) about your headstone. They might pay for it and inscribe with keys dates about your military service. Put this information, including process steps to achieve it, with your other end of life papers.

If you want to have military honors at your funeral, then have all the important information on who to contact kept with your Will to make it easier on your family. Be sure you know who will receive the folded flag as well. My mother watched many friends and family receive flags during WWII and didn't feel she could stand it when my father finally passed away. We solved the concern by having the flag given to my sister who was not only the oldest child but also retired military. It meant a lot to her and eased my mother's grief. Talk to your family and understand their feelings before finalizing your decisions.

If you aren't ingrained in the military life and lose a military family member, a comrade, the VA (Veterans Administration), or superior officer can provide you information on who to contact to make the process of closure easier. They will be there to help you know what the traditions are for the specific branch of the military. The military is a close-knit community of professionals there to help at any time, even when one of their own passes.

Obituary Or Death Announcements

Be sure to post an obituary in the local paper when close family members pass away. Then keep a copy. It's useful for insurance claims as well as family history. If you don't want to pay for the paper, have the funeral home post something on the location for the memorial service. Keep those to provide not only proof but also family records information for future generations.

Obituaries generally give a full name, age at death and mention other family members. If a spouse already passed, they should be mentioned as well. If you don't want flowers, ask for donations for favorite charities. These articles normally include key organizations or hobbies the deceased enjoyed. You don't have to mention the cause of death. If the funeral is private, say so or include information on the services if you want to let anyone come that knew the person.

With the rise in popularity for cremation more people are scheduling life celebrations / memorials at a later time. Be sure to find out how to reach people about the date of this delayed service. Social media is helpful, but with all the filters they might miss a general announcement. (As shocking as this sounds, some people don't get on social media so be sure you know how to reach them as well.)

Make A Memory Others Will Appreciate

It only takes a minute to make a memory. Write a thank-you note and touch someone in a way that a social media message can never accomplish. Pregnant? Write letters to your future child for key dates while you're pregnant: 16th, 18th, 21st, wedding. Include not only your dreams for them, but also notes on what you remember about your own life on those dates.

Did someone you know lose a person in their life? Wait a few months then write a simple note including a memory with a simple *thinking of you* message. Grief doesn't end in thirty days and good memories are always welcomed.

Want to make a more lasting memory during a funeral? Have cards or a book for guests to write their favorite stories about the deceased. If they are related, have them include how they're related. Now you have something to share with others in the family after the flood of emotions and people subside.

Another future thinking idea is to start a letter to your grandchild when they're born. Add something to it either yearly or on special dates. Have them receive it the day before they get married, when they graduate, or maybe just for their 25th birthday. The memories will touch them and keep you forever in their heart, even if you pass on before that date.

Get a photo album or digital photo file set up. Add three to five pictures for each year to remind you of special memories. Add notes with the year and you'll create a treasure to be passed down from generation to generation. If it's a digital file be sure to have a backup. Be sure to tell others in your life where to find these memories in case you pass suddenly. They will find comfort in looking through your memories.

TRAINING YOUR BRAIN

When you graduated from high school and / or college, you swore you were through with learning. You just knew you were fully prepared to tackle life without all those math, English, or science classes. I hate to tell you this, but in life, you never stop learning. In fact, they say that challenging your brain keeps it healthier meaning it might help you out a bit longer.

You might not be taking formal education classes, but new technology, new software for work, even some new thing to cook means you have to learn. And sometimes you think back on school and just wish you'd written down that math formula to cut down that recipe, remembered what not to mix in chemistry class so you don't blow up the house with cleaning supplies, even how to use that rule in physics to help you move something.

Sometimes your day job wants you to take a certification course on that new technology so you can use it properly. Other times you might be curious and want to learn something. (Hey, it's possible.) Or maybe you're considering going back to school to learn a new industry so you can get in a better paying job.

Don't get in a funk thinking about learning and wishing you'd remember all the stuff you shoved into the darkest corners of your mind the day you graduated. My best friend gave me a great list of things to add to my learning list that comes in handy. You might want to bookmark this section and keep it close by at work or when learning. This is a great reference list.

Math Tricks

If you're in school this list of simple math tips will help you in all sorts of ways. If you're not in school, this will help you get through some of life's challenges. If you know one not listed here, share it on social media with everyone. People appreciate help with life and work.

- When doing a math problem, remember to use the order of operations to guide you in solving the problem. If you don't do the calculations in the correct order you will get a different answer. PEMDAS is the word to guide the order.
  - **P**arenthesis
  - **E**xponents
  - **M**ultiply
  - **D**ivide
  - **A**dd
  - **S**ubtract
- Example of PEMDAS: 2*5+4. Following the correct order to Multiple before Adding
  - 2*5 = 10 + 4 = 14.
  - Without the rule 5+4 = 9 *2 = 18.
  - 14 is the correct answer.
- After the order of operations, work left to right.
- When working on a math problem using a formula, actually write out the formula then replace it with the actual numbers. This keeps the errors down.
  - Example A=L x W, A=2 x 5, A=10.
- Word problems. Read it carefully. Draw or write out what you do know. If you are missing information, write out a letter to represent it.

Use the clues to solve the unknown quantities. Check the answer by plugging the numbers back in.
- When working multiplication, division, and addition, make sure your numbers are lined up so you don't make careless errors.
- Is your answer not on the list? Check back over your work. It is common to subtract instead of divide and add instead of multiply out of habit.
- Make an estimate of your answer, then work the problem. If you expected 1200 and came out with 120, you may have missed a decimal or lined up the numbers incorrectly.
- Word problem vocabulary.
  - Per means divided by.
  - Quotient and ratio both mean to divide.
  - Difference between means subtract.
- Divide by 9 to uncover transposition errors or where you left off a 0 at the end of the number. When you divide by 9 you should come out with an even number and no decimal points. If not, you have an error. Ex: you wrote 325 instead of 352 or used 14 instead of 140.
- In bookkeeping, being a penny off between debits and credits is not just a penny. You have an error somewhere. Review the numbers again.

Memory Tricks

Many people struggle to remember that critical bit of information when needed for a test. There are many ways to remember something including writing it a gazillion times, or reciting it until you wish you never want to hear about it again. I recommend you start by thinking about the type of learner you are. Are you an auditory (music or spoken), visual (see it), or physical (activity) learner?

There are professionals who will help you discover your learning style but some people picked up on what worked for them as they grew up. This is how my friends and I classified the information. Auditory people find that reading out loud or singing something provides the interaction for their brain to remember something. Others must see things like reading words or viewing pictures. A physical learner needs to interact with the information like touching a sculpture or making a graph. Writing information out by hand can help these types make the connection.

You might find that a blend of more than one learning style is really your style. I'm an auditory and physical learner. Hearing it and writing it down is like waving a red flag in front of a bull. It tells my brain to pay attention.

Trying a mixture of methods allows you to find one that fits the topic and your style. And a bit of variety is always nice. For those willing to explore new things here are some memory tricks that could save your hand or your brain cells.

- Put it to music. People can remember songs from 20-30-40 years or more ago when they hear a tune. As a child, you learned your alphabet by singing it. As an adult, you'll find that songs can work just as well. (Bet you can still do that now!)
- Teach someone else what you learn. Recalling it and explaining it to someone else helps clear up any doubts in your mind.
- Write it over, and over. If you are a visual learner, this burns it into your mind. (Yeah, the hand might hurt a bit, but it might be the best fit for you.)
- Repeat it out loud multiple times. This is a great way for auditory learners to remember something. Some will adjust their reading of the material to fit a poetry style or rap to help them feel the words.
- Relate it to something you already know. For instance, if you already know about basketball, and you are learning about angles, insert the angles into your basketball shots. This can be a fun way to learn geometry. Pies or cookies are a great way to learn fractions.
- Use mnemonic devices to remember things. This means using a pattern of letters, words, or other associations that act as a short cut for the thing. Here are a couple of examples.
  - I want a HOME on a Great Lake. The Great Lakes are HOMES - Huron, Ontario, Michigan, Erie, and Superior.
  - Please Excuse My Dear Aunt Sally (PEMDAS) is a mnemonic device used to remember the order of math operations.

Parenthesis, **E**xponents, **M**ultiply, **D**ivide, **A**dd, then **S**ubtract.

Reading Comprehension / Analysis Tips

I never did well on the reading comprehension section of those standardized tests growing up. I learned later in life that I tended to get easy puzzles wrong and harder ones right so maybe that had something to do with it. I wonder if I'd had this list back then if I could've done better on that ACT.

My day job requires me to solve problems and I use several of these things when looking at data or writing instructions for others to help unlock the answers. So, don't look at this just as a list of reading tips. Look at it as a way to analyze things.
- Glance over the questions. See what you will be looking for in your reading. If you are solving a problem in life, write down the questions you have to solve.
- Read the full passage with the questions in mind. If you can, underline things that stand out to you during the reading.
- Make yourself interested in the passage - pay attention to what you're reading. You will "get it" better if you make your mind think you are interested in it.
- Look for keywords. Be sure you understand what those words mean to the overall topic.
- Discard answers that are obviously wrong. Things that are the opposite of questions or off-topic of the questions.
- Look for context. Don't just read the sentence you are being asked about. Look at the sentence before and after it for things that would change the interpretation. Words like *does* verses

doesn't can be misinterpreted when reading in a hurry.
- If you are struggling to stay focused, read aloud (quietly). This is especially true for auditory learners.
- When teaching sight words to children make it a game. Cut index cards in half and write the same word on two cards. Do this for all the words. Now mix the cards and spread them out on a table or the floor. Ask the child to turn over two cards at a time. As they turn each card face up, they must say the words out loud. If the cards match, they get set aside. If they don't match, turn them face down and try again.

Letters, Words - Vocabulary

I didn't get nor retain all that Latin stuff in school, but these word tips come in handy on a regular basis. Have one, not on the list? Post it to social media and help everyone. Don't forget to tag me, too!

- If you don't know the meaning of a word in a sentence, look for context clues. The word context is a great example. Here it means giving a clue to the meaning of the sentence.
- Say the word out loud. Sometimes it will activate your memory of hearing the word used in another sentence that helps clarify the usage.
- If you don't know the word, look at the pieces of the word for something familiar. For instance, say the word is ambulatory. *Ambul* in the word like an ambulance moves you. Look for a word in the definition having to do with moving.
- Here are a few other prefix words to help you untangle the meanings:
    - "co" means joint or multiple, like co-pilot means helping the pilot fly.
    - "de" means off, down or away from, like de-frost means to take the frost off.
    - "un" means not or reversal, like un-cover means to remove the cover.
    - "bi" means two, like bi-monthly is twice a month. (Yep those pesky prefixes might tell you how often you get paid.)
- Read! It improves your vocabulary.

More Tips For Learning

As if all the lists before this aren't enough. My best friend and I let loose with a few more things that can help, including a few to get you through those boring work meetings. Remember learning is important to keeping your brain healthy for the long term.
- Always be prepared. If it's a written test, bring extra pencils. Ask in advance if they allow calculators, scrap paper, etc.
- If it's possible to study for the test, DO IT! Study with a friend or family member part of the time. They can add a different view or tip on the subject even relating it to something else in your life that helps you remember it.
- If possible, take practice tests to build your confidence and familiarity with the way the test works. If there aren't any practice tests, make your own. Get a few other friends in the class to write out the questions. Then mix the cards up and have a game night to prepare for the test. If someone misses a question, then put a penny in the jar. At the end of the night, use the money for a treat.
- Make your own flashcards with questions on the front and answers on the back OR a set of cards for questions and answers. Mix up the cards and see how many you can match correctly. This is another one good to do alone or with friends.
- Rule out obviously wrong answers first.
- Eat a meal high in protein the morning of a big test or meeting so the mind won't wander because the tummy is growling.

- Remember to stop and breathe during the test. Your brain needs oxygen to work and it will help you slow your brain down allowing you to think about the answers.
- Drink water. Hydration makes your bodywork better including your brain. It's also very helpful in long meetings to keep you focused on the meeting and not drifting off to sleep.
- Be on time. Running late puts adrenaline in your body that makes it harder to focus. Being late for a meeting can mean missing the opening / point of the meeting purpose that makes everything else make sense.
- Read the instructions and questions thoroughly. My mom was a teacher and each year she gave her new students a test telling them to read all the instructions first. She made them very long but if they did as she instructed, the students found out they only needed to answer two questions on the test. Teachers love this tactic.

LIFE LESSONS REVISITED

When my children were young, we lived in a wonderful neighborhood filled with old-fashioned beliefs that we were not just neighbors, we were family. Young, old, single, married, multi-raced, all together - a wonderful family. We guided, encouraged, punished, and taught our children together. We traded great cooking like a loaf of homemade bread for a homemade pound cake. (Spoiler alert - we used a bread machine.) When we picked turnip greens, another would cook them with a big smoked turkey leg and split the resulting goodness with us.

When I couldn't teach my daughter to tie her shoes, my wonderful neighbor did it in ten minutes. When our son reached the age to explore fire, a firefighter neighbor had that difficult discussion for us, teaching him the deadly danger and important responsibilities that accompanied fire. In turn, we taught kids about playing safely near the busier street we lived on and showed them how to deal with a new bully that moved into the neighborhood.

Radio, TV, the internet, social media, and cell phones have pushed their way into our lives distracting us from family and friends, as well as discouraging people from getting involved with others. We've traded in helping to guide all children for being afraid to discipline our own fearing public scorn. I say these things to remind you that along the way, we've lost some important lessons that need to find their way back into our lives.

As a child, you heard "say please" or "say thank you" over, and over. These phrases are on the early lessons list that parents follow when raising children. As teenagers, your mind begins to explore new concepts that generally includes a compelling desire to rebel against rules. Once you hit what we now call "adulting time" or the real working world, you need a quick refresher course to put you on the right path. A path that impacts the impression people have of you that can make or break the opportunities life presents. Let's get started.

Thx, Thanks, Thank You-The Beginning Of The End

Texting, talking, writing, email, or even picking out an appropriate card to say it for you, "Thank You" are two words that seem to make people stumble. We mumble it, forget to say it, or use it sparingly as if it was an expensive new toy.

Some say conversation is an art and maybe it is, but you can count on one thing. Using the words Thank You changes the perception of an encounter by emphasizing that you've received some kind of training in the art of social graces. Encounters with other humans involve a never-ending cycle of conversation techniques that, like a good book, include a beginning, a middle, and an end. Used to show gratitude before departing, Thank You normally occurs at the end of an exchange. It can even be used to politely say you don't want something. "Thank you, but not right now."

However, you need to use it. I challenge you to use it. The use of social graces disrupts angry customers, puts a smile on faces of all ages, and elevates the positive perception of the user. If you want to boost your perception after a job interview, send a thank you email or card with a handwritten note to the person / people who interviewed you. It can make the difference in getting hired in some companies.

If you want to touch someone, send a handwritten thank-you note. This goes a long way with those over fifty and can disrupt the perception someone under fifty has of you. Writing a note doesn't have to be hard. Address the person by name. Mention the event you are thanking them for and where possible include how that event impacted you.

Working with a local publisher, I spent some time leading a group that taught seminars on how to write. Several of us received a wonderful thank you note from a participant in the class. To say we were over the moon getting the note is an understatement. Following the classical note style, it used my name, thanked me for leading the seminar, and closed by saying how what she learned that would help her writing career.

If you're sending flowers, food, or another gift to carry your thank you message, be sure to include a handwritten card even if only a line or two of copy. The gift will be remembered far longer with the card.

Thank you for taking the time to explore this topic with me.

Please - One Word To Open Many Doors

Used as an adverb, this word transforms a request from sounding like an order to a polite question. A word that allows the requested person to grant your request, offer an alternate option or turn down your request, all while keeping the situation civil. Like thank you, it quickly broadcasts a positive impression of the user to others. In today's busy world with text style communication, this word acts as a speed bump. Catching people's attention with *please* sets the tone for a change in the conversation to a friendly and interactive encounter.

In addition to changing the tone of the conversation, this one word raises the level of respect in the situation by demonstrating your willingness to be polite. That's not to say that using the word with an angry or sarcastic tone, won't result in a different outcome. Even the nicest question said in the wrong tone can set off a catastrophic course of events you hadn't intended. So, remember to watch your tone of voice when making the request… please.

Ma'am Isn't Just For Kids

Respect for others has never gone out of style, unlike the popularity of using yes ma'am or yes sir. The hardest thing about using this phrase is getting comfortable hearing it said. When little kids use it, you think "sweet kid." Hearing the phrase used by a member of the military reminds you how ingrained respect for others is in their way of life.

As a twenty-something grabbing fast food, it can make you feel a bit creeped out when the kid or older worker behind the register says "yes, ma'am" to you. Something about those simple words makes you blush, mumble, and try to get away quickly. But why? Does it make us feel old or are we just nervous about the use of the respectful term? Maybe we just don't know how to answer this phrase. It's easy. Smile and say thank you. Make the person feel proud to say it to the next person.

Opening Doors To Civility

Opening the door for others is not only a sign of good manners, but it also says you are a polite person. In a world where the hustle and bustle of life makes people a bit testy, small gestures bring a smile to many faces. Momma always told us to open doors for those older than us. It was a sign of respect for the knowledge they held at their age.

Ladies, while mom always said that gentlemen should open doors for you, you should always defer to the age rule when in doubt about who opens the door. Saying thank you for the open door with a genuinely happy smile completes the experience in a positive light for everyone.

Civility doesn't have to stop with doors. Good manners and a warm smile can turn a bad day into a good one for most people. When you're happy share it with the world.

Smiles Go A Long Way

There are a few simple things you can do that pay off in ways you might not expect. The first is a smile. When you walk by a mirror or reflective glass, look at yourself. If you naturally have a smile on then pat yourself on the back. If you don't, then practice it. A smile says you are happy, having fun, or maybe into a bit of mischief, but people will start a conversation in a more positive tone when the person is smiling.

Sad or angry faces have speakers preparing for you to snarl or yell at them. And if you really needed help from the person you might find more no's coming your way than yes's. I've heard that people who smile a lot are not only happier but also live longer. However, the song says the good die young so I make no claims to your life expectancy, only that it can be helpful. Keep Smiling and get the world to smile with you.

Etiquette

DO NOT TYPE IN ALL CAPS - this is considered yelling at someone in anger. Your work emails are not social media. Don't use those LOL, THX, etc.

And if someone on social media is asking for information on something, don't say, "can't you just Google it?" Consider that they are asking for someone to give them a "trusted" source for the information. Additionally, just because they can write a post on social media, it does not mean they are good with internet searches. There are a lot of scammer sites and misinformation on the world wide web (www) and not everyone knows how to filter those out.

What I consider the proper use of Facebook Messages is a thing that can send me off in a grumpy mood if used incorrectly. (Hey, I never said I was perfect.). I periodically receive things through Facebook Messages that I feel belong in someone's news feed and not a private message. Things like pass this on today or something will happen, or here is my thought for the day. In my view, a Private Message is to tell me something you don't want others on social media to know. Using Private Message to invite certain people to a private event that is what I consider a proper use along with sharing your phone number or email address in order to keep them private.

Sending me videos of political messages, bible quotes, or don't have bad luck junk stuff, is like screaming, "I don't know how to use Facebook." Sometimes the message is also sent to a group of people and not to me individually. I am, at most times, tolerant of the person and will send a nice message to keep me off all these things. Most of them reply sorry because they made a mistake and it's no problem. However, when one person replied with a snooty answer they were immediately blocked.

Remember that private messages are many times set to feed to a person's cell phone popping a notification sound when received. Like many of my friends, we're all out there trying to make a living. Interrupting a work meeting because you used Private Message to share a silly meme could get someone fired. So be polite and limit your use of the Facebook Private Message feature.

Flirting

When flirting with a girl (or guy) be sure you don't embarrass yourself! That seems like an easy thing to say but most men will tell you it's hard to do. My son learned this lesson at the early age of four. We were having lunch with friends in a McDonald's restaurant when he began to flirt with the cute little girl in the next booth. Now before you doubt the ability of a four-year-old to flirt, let me tell you he had blonde hair, vivid blue eyes, and eyelashes that made every girl jealous.

Flirting started by tilting his head slightly to one side, slowly drawing up an enticing smile, and sealing the deal by batting his eyes. Most girls fell instantly for this little game (and many adults too!) This time he turned around and put his head on his hand resting an elbow on the back of the booth. As he stared at the girl and began his flirt, his elbow slid to the right, into the space between the wall and the booth back. He was stuck. That flirting look quickly transitioned into panic.

The situation tickled me and my best friend. We began to giggle while slowly getting up to move the other two children we had with us out of the way. With help from her dad tugging on the plastic seat my son's arm quickly popped out remedying the situation. As we thanked the girl's dad for helping with the tug and began to put the kids back in their places, we found the whole thing even more amusing because the backup plan was to call the fire department from across the street, to extract him. Of course, we would have to explain he was stuck because he was flirting.

My son went from flirt to panic to embarrassment and he was only four. Unfortunately for him, the young lady lost interest. I'm sad to say, we didn't get to see any cute firefighters either. Ah, the sacrifices we make for our kids.

Flirting is supposed to be the way you indicate interest in another person. However, some people flirt with everyone they meet leaving the recipient confused about how to interpret the message. Do you really have an interest in a relationship with them? Do you think this is how to get your way on something you need from them? Flirting can make others very uncomfortable.

If you aren't sure if you're a flirt, ask your best friend. If the answer is yes, then pay attention to how you interact with others. Look at yourself in the mirror or get your best friend to help you identify your flirty moves. Narrow down the flirting to the person you want to attract so they don't miss the signal to them among all the others you project. Practice not using these moves with others and before long it will be a great new communication habit.

More Basic Thoughts

Here are a few other things I heard from mom and other adults. Some of these are about making the world a better place and others are just to make you a better person. Knowing my parents lived through World War II meant that many times, they had limits on things like food staples or metals as supplies had to be diverted to support the troops. They lived life a bit differently not wasting anything and that view was pushed down to the young children they raised.

I hope these points will help you with your habits makeover and maybe help you control your impact on the world as we know it.
- If you drop it, pick it up. If you spill it, clean it up. Be neat.
- Finish your food or clean your plate. There are hungry children in the world and your body needs the nutrients.
- Don't put food on your plate that you can't finish. It's about waste again.
- Turn off the light when you leave the room. Save energy.
- Turn on the light if you're reading. Help your eyes.
- Try to fix it rather than replace it. Saves money and landfill space.

All in all, these are Life Lessons - please, thank you, help others, smile, pick up behind yourself, open doors for people, say hello. It doesn't matter if you believe in God, a higher power, or just fate, being polite and helpful to others will always come back to serve you well in the future.

Life's lessons affect us every day in many ways. Try a few of these and see what impact they have on your life. Teach others these lessons and you make the world a better place to live.

Life Lessons Revisited | 165

Making The World Better

I am all about making life nicer. Angry people cause stress and disrupt everything. This is a short list of easy things people can do to make the world better for everyone.

- **Good attitude.** Talking to yourself when angry or frustrated, allows you to work through the emotions without affecting others. Sometimes it will keep you from saying something you don't really mean that can set off a string of bad events.
- **Smile.** It's free, doesn't cause you pain, and can disrupt an upset person. Happy people might even live a bit longer if you believe some of the doctors out there.
- **Turn signals.** Yep, I said this before. It comes on the car at no extra expense. Using these correctly can reduce your chances to be in a wreck that will spin life out of control. Make this a habit and do it today.
- **Glass half full.** We all have a bad day where we can't seem to be positive about anything, but don't let that be your everyday life. Keep in mind that things could be worse and that whatever happened it is only a speed bump in your life. Try to be positive and look at things like the glass is half full instead of empty.
- **Opening doors**. Repeating this reminder to take a moment to be polite opening doors, or saying please, and thank you. It's free. Why not do it?

- **Letting cars merge or turn ahead of you**. If everyone considered the lessons they learned in kindergarten about being nice, the world would be better. Let other cars merge into traffic using the every other car process. If there are several people at a four-way stop, motion for someone else to go first. You might be in a hurry but the extra couple of seconds could be the difference in a good day for you or someone else. Take the time to be nice.
- **Keep the world neat**. When you're out and about and you see trash dropped, pick it up and throw it away. When you're in a restaurant and the bathroom is out of toilet paper, tell them. If someone splashed water all over the floor, tell someone who can clean it up. These little things will come back to you because you've set the tone for others to see how easy it is to make a positive impact on the world.

COOKING TO LIVE

Eating out in the city is usually easy but not always cheap. If you live a bit further out then you have fewer options on finding other people to cook for you. And cooking for just yourself can present challenges, especially if you want to eat a bit healthier or follow a special diet. If you want to take on the cooking challenge then let's learn a bit about it.

First, you should consider that cooking is something to explore and have fun with it. Food can be an expression of your personality, culinary preferences, and a way to save money. Like most things, a bit of planning goes a long way to save money especially if don't like eating the same thing for a week because you made too much. Cooking for two sounds easy but it provides another set of likes and dislikes to work around. If one or both parties are flexible it won't be a problem.

Don't be afraid of cooking. Just like walking you should start with baby steps. This section of the book will take some of the mystery out helping you get started.

What You Like

Start by making a list of foods you like to eat. Include simple things like scrambled eggs or fresh vegetables, more complex things like meatloaf or casseroles, and be sure to cover the spectrum of meats, vegetable dishes, even desserts.

Now divide the list into things you know how to make and those you don't. If you like something and can make it, you just need to understand how to adjust portions or ingredients to fit your needs. For the items you like but don't know how to make, pick one or two and find someone you know to teach you how to make the item. In return, they get to stay for dinner.

Want to have more fun? Have a few friends over for a cooking night. Plan a menu and pick the friends, then gather in someone's kitchen and help each other learn to cook. Encourage everyone to try something new and expand your taste buds together.

Planning Your Yummies

Now that you know what you like you need to group menu ideas that use similar ingredients. This allows you to buy something like chicken or your favorite veggies and make a couple of different dishes. Take special note of things you can easily freeze as these bonus dishes allow you to cook once and portion off a couple of other meals to get out later.

If you want to eat healthier, they say to work with fresh ingredients and not the pre-packaged stuff found in the center of the store. If it's a pre-made, one-skillet dish, check the labels and compare them to your eating goals. Frozen is also supposed to be better than canned but not as healthy as fresh. If you don't care what's in it, then go wild!

Let's look at a couple of easy things to make. Fresh mixed green salads that include spinach leaves gives you a flexible base. Grill or cook some chicken with a drop or so of olive or coconut oil. Then chop it up into bite-size pieces. These two basics can be turned into several dishes using a variety of spices to give you different flavors.

Here are a few ideas to get you started.
- Grilled chicken on a salad is first and easy.
- Use a tortilla as the base, layer on some of the salad or chicken, add some spicy mustard and roll into a wrap.
- Using a piece of frozen garlic bread or your favorite artisan choice, pick out some spinach

from the salad greens and layer on the bread with chicken and some chopped fresh veggies. Bake or eat fresh.
- Make some whole wheat pasta. Toss in the chicken and some Italian dressing then top with some fresh spinach, or veggies. When cooking with whole wheat pasta, remember that you might want to lengthen your cooking time just a bit and that it might take a bit for your taste buds to accept the difference. We love the whole wheat thin spaghetti done like this.

Look at your favorite recipes and find ways to make them healthier. Swap tomato sauce or paste out with diced tomatoes. Finely chop fresh vegetables like zucchini, yellow squash, onions, bell peppers, and mushrooms, then add your spaghetti seasonings to slip veggies into your favorite Italian meals.

My freezer usually has containers or zip closed bags with pre-chopped mixtures of zucchini, yellow squash, onions, bell peppers, mushrooms, or other veggies in different combinations. When I start cooking it's easy to grab some, zap a moment in the microwave and add them to anything. Now meatloaf and spaghetti have hidden veggies, leftover rice can be transformed into a stir fry, or I can slip it into my favorite chili recipe to boost the healthy and extend the dish.

If you are a veggie hater, try finely chopping the veggies before adding to a dish. These little tricks have worked for years with my family and my daughter was the definition of picky growing up.

Adjusting The Amounts

Recipes are a combination of specific amounts of ingredients. Cutting the quantities in half or doubling sounds easy (if you get the math) but wait till you have to find a use for ½ a can of leftover something. This is where the planning comes in. Now when you adjust the amounts look for another recipe to use the leftover ingredients so you don't have any waste. If you find you don't have a use for the item, make the full dish and freeze some or share the extra food with a friend.

Need ½ an egg? Use egg substitute or whip the leftover into a breakfast treat to put on a bagel for the next morning. Need just a little of a veggie like celery, mushrooms, or onions? Buy what you need off the salad bar at the grocery to control the leftovers.

There are a lot of ideas online to substitute things like apple sauce for oil, or different types of sugars or flours to make recipes healthier. Some of these make cutting or doubling a recipe easier. Try playing around with things but don't forget to write down your changes. When you get a dish you like, you want to be able to make it again.

Recipe Basics

With the recipe in hand, you're excited about making that cool looking dish but the recipe suddenly looks like a foreign language or computer code. Don't panic. Let's talk about some of the basics of cooking that will make this easier.

Most recipes are divided into two parts: ingredients and instructions. Read the instructions first. Sometimes they contain tips on how to prepare the ingredients or they give insight into the pots, pans, and utensils needed to fix the dish. Be sure you have everything. Then review the ingredients list making notes for buying anything you don't have on hand before beginning to cook.

Measure all the ingredients out in the order they are listed to be sure you have enough of each item before you start mixing things together. Then put away all the ingredient containers to give you more room to work. If you'll need to bake it in the oven, stop and turn it on. Ovens need time to reach the cooking temperature (it's called preheating).

Now layout all the utensils and pans needed. Stop and fill the sink with hot soapy water. This lets you drop stuff into soak when no longer needed.

> **Caution:** Watch for special recipe instructions that say chill the bowl. You'll need to allow some extra pre-planning for instructions like this.

If you have to prepare the pan with shortening, flour, non-stick spray, parchment paper or cupcake liners, do that next. This allows you to have everything ready to go when you finish mixing. Now you're ready to follow the instructions and cook something yummy! (Dang! Now I'm hungry again.)

What Size Is That?

People who cook a lot rattle off words and think everyone knows what things mean. If you don't know a term, look it up while you're reading the instructions the first time. If you're making a recipe from a friend in England, you'll probably need to convert it to American measures. We use ounces and they use liters. As I am not great at conversions I'll stick to American terms for this discussion.

First off there is a difference in measuring liquid and dry ingredients in larger quantities. Measuring cups for dry ingredients are normally plastic with a handle and come pre-sized. Look for 1 cup, ½ cup, and 1/3 cup all coming as a set. Liquid measures are usually see-through containers with the sizes marked on the sides. These may include marks in cup sizes and ounces.

> **Tip:** Don't panic about the fractions. It will match those in the recipe so you know what size measure you need to pour out.

Shortening, sugar, pecans, and chopped vegies are all measured as dry ingredients. Oil, milk, water, and wine are all measured in a liquid measure. When a recipe shows "c" by a number it means cup like ½ c. You have to know whether the ingredient is measured in a dry or liquid container. These are the larger and primary ingredients in a recipe making up the bulk of the finished product. Just fill to the matching line and you're done.

Teaspoons (tsp) and tablespoons (tbsp) terms are for measuring small amounts. A standard measuring spoon set has 1/8 tsp, ¼ tsp, ½ tsp, 1 tsp, and 1 tbs. (Note there are 4 teaspoons in a tablespoon.) This spoon set is used for both liquid or dry ingredients. Ingredients measured by the tsp or tbs are generally spices, baking powders, salts, and other additives that either add flavor or creates a food reaction like making bread rise.

People who cook often might keep a measuring cup in their flour and sugar. I keep a ¼ measure in my sugar and a ½ cup measure in my flour. That's because most of my recipes are a multiple of that size and it is always handy. For example, if I need 2 cups of flour, I fill the ½ cup measure 4 times (4 x ½ = 2). To do this you might need to have a second set of measuring cups and of course airtight containers to store the ingredients safely away from bugs and air.

> **Tip:** I'd like to give a shout out to Tupperware. They not only have wonderful containers that seal with an easy burp, but they have a chart that tells you what container will hold things like 4 lbs. of sugar or 5 lbs. of flour, or a box of cereal.
>
> When I started setting up my home my group of friends took turns hosting a series of parties to help with discounts on our favorite kitchen stuff like Tupperware or Pampered Chef. This saves money, lets you have fun, and fixes problems in the kitchen!

Spring What?

Like people, pans have a variety of names like Bundt, sheet pan, springform, even tube. (No, springform pans have nothing to do with jumping or launching things into the air.) These special pans allow you to remove the sides from the finished product before removing your creation from the bottom. This protects a delicate finished product during the un-panning process. Now you can slip it off the parchment paper or run a knife between the pan bottom and the finished product to separate the pieces while holding the desired shape.

Bundt pans have cool lines in the pans and a hole in the middle. They're designed to cook thicker / larger cakes and look great with a sauce drizzled over the top. 9x13, 9x9, 8x8 and round pans are generally used to make a multi-layered dessert. With a knife or wire, you can even split each layer of a pan into two layers for more yummy filling layer options.

Sheet pans or cookie sheets come in a variety of sizes but all have very low sides. You can bake cookies or "sheet cakes" on these, brown those French fries or tater tots, even use them to make grilled cheese or to brown your favorite garlic bread creation.

Soufflé or quiche dishes are normally ceramic designed to be effective for cooking, yet stylish enough to double as a serving dish. Pie pans are traditionally round with low sides and while perfect for cooking pies, you can use them for baking cinnamon rolls or reheating leftovers.

Saucepans are the ones used on top of the stove designed for cooking liquid items. Available in different sizes and colors, they also come with lids. Since most have a plastic handle, I don't recommend putting them in the dishwasher too often or the handles won't last as long as the pan.

Skillets or frying pans are preferred for sautéing veggies or frying foods. I recommend investing in a quality set of saucepans and skillets. Be sure you get at least one with a lid. The higher quality versions will last a long time and usually provide a great even cooking surface as long as you take care of them. Don't put the hot pan in water or you risk warping the bottom. Let them cool before washing. Since many come with non-stick surfaces, be sure to invest in some non-metal utensils to protect the cooking finish. These days the utensils come in a variety of colors to fit your mood or kitchen designs.

A mixing bowl is just a bowl large enough to stir your ingredients together without spilling over. It can be metal, plastic, or even glass. These also come in sets with a couple of different sizes to fit your needs. My favorite is an old aluminum bowl handed down from my grandmother. There are some treasured childhood memories of her mixing things in the bowl and I know she is helping me cook every time I use her bowl.

You don't have to buy all this to start cooking, but if the recipe calls for one, you'll need to include it in the pre-cooking shopping.

Kitchen Gadgets

Don't think that home repair people are the only ones with cool tools. People who like to cook have a variety of neat things to use and can be just as particular about their choices. Knives have names like peeling, chef's, boning, cleaver, bread, or butcher. Mix in graters, choppers, whisks, strainers, sifters, and squeezers, and soon you have a drawer full of stuff. How do you know what to buy?

A couple types and sizes of knives are great for anything and I love my little electronic chopper. A strainer comes in handy for cooking pasta or draining fruits and vegetables. After that, what you need depends on what you're cooking. Any time you're making a new recipe be sure to read through it, looking for any kitchen gadgets you might need to buy while you're getting the ingredients.

If you aren't sure about how much you'll use the special gadget in the recipe, maybe borrow any special tools from a friend for the first time. Then if you don't like the recipe, you don't have another gadget taking up space in the cabinet or drawers.

If you begin cooking specialty foods like Italian, candy making, or baking, you'll find additional kitchen tools needed that are unique to that choice. Pasta machines, candy thermometers, citrus peelers, even rolling pins could all be part of your new passion. If you want to try something new, see if the local cooking stores offer classes. This lets you try out new things and specialty tools before investing.

Keeping It Safe To Eat

Food does go bad. The pizza from last month's party may not be safe to eat three weeks later. Most people get this concept especially if there is a soft green fuzz covering the slices. Canned and packaged foods usually carry a *Use By* or *Sell By* date to guide you when you can't remember when you bought it.

Leftovers confuse most people. You'll find them doing internet searches on how long to keep that leftover casserole or steak hoping it will be safe to have for dinner tonight. When in doubt toss is out! (Food poisoning is not worth the risk. Trust me!)

Here is my refrigerator plan. Cook meals on Sunday or Monday and eat on them all week. This way I hope to have it all gone or nearly gone by the start of the next week. Besides, I have to clean out the refrigerator before I can cook food for the next week. The back up to the plan is that if you don't know how long it has been in there then toss it.

There are a few other tips that can improve the safety of your food.
- Watch for cross contamination. Do you love peanut butter and jelly? I bet you use one spoon in both jars. Pull out the peanut better before the jelly. Jelly is a refrigerator item and peanut butter isn't. So, if you leave the jelly in the peanut butter it can spoil. (Danger!)
- Don't cut raw meats then other foods with the same knife. Get a clean knife or wash it.

- Clean cutting boards and counter tops with soap between uses, especially after cutting chicken, fish, or pork.
- Read the labels on how to properly thaw or cook frozen foods. This includes that holiday turkey. If you do it wrong, you can get sick. (If the family gets food poisoning during the holidays they will never forget. And they will remind you every year!)
- I know you want to eat healthy but take time to wash those fruits and vegetables. The nightly news regularly runs stories reporting listeria outbreaks. Don't be the next headline.
- Take time every few months to clean out the refrigerator. You'll discover moldy things, spills, and little bits of stuff. Clean the shelves and walls with soapy water and enjoy the fresh feeling again.

WHERE YOU LIVE

We've talked about keeping your home organized to improve functionality and ways to make it easier to keep it clean. These concepts apply no matter where you live – with your parents / children, an apartment, a house, a trailer, a cabin, a boat, even a retirement home. What we haven't covered is deciding where to live and things that impact that decision.

These days very few people are born, live, and die in one place. That means making decisions several times during your life, for different reasons, maybe during stressful times, and impacted by others in your world. Many things go into the decision to move like paperwork, the physical move, and the impact of your decisions on others in your life. Let's dig into some of the thing's you'll need to think about.

Assessing The Options

The list of places you can live varies based on several factors like do you live in the city, a small town, or maybe the country. Of course, your income and the cost of the place you're considering are also at the top of the decision tree. After all, if you don't have enough money to pay for it then the place isn't part of your options list even if you *just gotta live there*.

Other factors can include roommates, spouses, pets, children, type or distance to work, your desire or ability to maintain the place, even the changing feeling of safety in your neighborhood. Maybe you've lived at home as part of a family of six all your life and you just want a place without anyone around at the end of each day. Or do you want a place that offers a social life to get you out of the house. Merging your life with a spouse or a roommate means you have to consider what the other person is looking for as well.

If you have a dog or other pets you might want a yard or at the very least a place that lets you keep your beloved Fido. If you have children then the rating of the local schools is important unless you're planning to pay for private school. Maybe you're allergic to grass so you don't want a yard.

If all this seems overwhelming it's time to break out the paper and pen and start a list. (Hey, I don't have a list for everything in the book!) Here is a list of questions to guide your decision tree.

- How many people will share the place? Translate that to the number of bedrooms and bathrooms needed.
- You like having all the bedrooms upstairs so no one sees you don't make the bed or maybe you need everything on one floor. If you're considering an apartment or renting a room from someone you'll need to decide if you want people living above or below you.
- Which of these amenities do you need? Yard, garage, outside storage, attic storage, swimming pool, dedicated office space, or playroom (for children or adults).
- Prioritize how important it is to be close to any of these items: school, work, church, stores, coffee shops, restaurants, doctors or hospitals.
- Think about what you do in your free time and if you need to be close to the mountains, lakes / rivers, running trails, a sports complex or even a specific type of gym.
- Decide if you want to buy or rent setting a budget amount to work with that will include all the related costs.

With your list in hand look at the options available in your area that fit your criteria. If you find several options rank them based on how they meet the criteria but don't rule anything out.

Go see each option in person. Looking at the options will uncover things not on the list that you suddenly find you care about. A big kitchen to cook in or a giant soaking tub, a patio for grilling out, even a retro design or ultra-modern feel can bring out the need to fight for a particular location. Happy hunting!

Buy, Rent, Lease

It's only money, or so they say. Knowing how much money you have to pay for a place to live is important but so is the choice between buying, renting or leasing. There are pros and cons each of these choices and many of the decisions were made with your lists in the *Assessing The Options* section.

Let's cover the options from a slightly different perspective. The short and long-term impact on your net worth. What is net worth? It is the total of all the cash plus the value of all those things you own minus any money you owe to others (think bills). The more you own the greater your net worth. Buying / owning a home is worth more to you than renting or leasing a place. Let's dig a bit deeper into these options and how they impact you.

Leasing is generally a longer-term commitment and may come with an option to put some of the money you pay toward eventually buying the place. If so, eventually you purchase the place and pay on the mortgage until you own it out right. Lease to own is not always the case so be sure you have a lawyer look at any contracts to be sure you understand your options. Always ask the length of the commitment and be sure you understand all out clauses in case you decide you hate the place and want to move.

Additionally, the lease contracts will spell out who pays for repairs. Unlike renting, it might fall on the leasee (you). If so, be sure to put money into your budget for the upkeep because failure to do so could cost you even more. And if you're leasing without the option to buy / own at the end remember any money you spend fixing it up helps the value for the owner, not you.

Maybe you are leaning toward renting. There are strong reasons for some people to rent. If you have poor credit then becoming a renter allows you to improve your score with only a short commitment and impact. Renters do have to pass a credit check and poor credit will limit your location options. However, these contracts are six or twelve-month commitments, not thirty years so as your credit improves you could move to a nicer place if you want.

Renting means someone else takes care of the repairs and their costs. Making changes to the paint, walls, or other structural parts is normally not allowed. It also means that if you don't like the place you can move in a short amount of time. Just give the proper notice, pack up, and move. However, this doesn't add to your net worth and you will continue to pay rent every month until you die.

Buying to own isn't for everyone and does take some preparation. Start by making sure you have a good credit score. (You know, that number you see on all the commercials telling you how important it is.) And by now you've figured out a budget and the basic criteria needed to find a place (lists!).

Buying is a long-term commitment. You can sell it and get out but you might not always get the most out of the transaction. The advantage to owing is that once you pay off the mortgage you own the place. Then your costs are tied to maintenance, insurance, and taxes which is normally a lot smaller number every month.

Buying also provides a couple of other options. First there can be a savings on your yearly federal taxes (see a tax person to see if it will help you). Secondly, when you've owned your home for awhile you can use some of the money you've paid on the cost of the house (equity) as another loan (home equity line of credit). This money can be used to fix up the house or cover those surprise home systems breakdowns. To have this option you'll need to qualify and have paid off a healthy part (20%+) of your loan. There can be fees and you will have to pay it back so watch your budget here as well.

So, in the end only you can choose which option is a fit for you. And life events can change which option is a fit at different times of your life. You could start out as a renter then buy, then return to renting. And yes, at any time during your life you can move in with family or others and they might not charge you anything for living there.

If you do get to move in for free, remember you impact their utilities, grocery budget, put more work on home equipment like washers and refrigerators, and that costs them money. Either occasionally chip in some money or offer to buy groceries or a couple of meals out in return for not paying rent. A free place to live is a great option if you need to pay off your bills and save some money.

For those newly emerging adults I recommend a compromise with the parents for a year or two extra time at home after college or trade training. Save your money and start out without so many struggles. It could be the difference between working two jobs or moving home again later because you got in over your head.

Remember, it's *only money* if you have more than you need. Very few people can ignore the impact money has on their lives. They say if you take care of the money it will take care of you. Choose how to spend it carefully. Then enjoy your decisions.

Surviving The Process

Buying, renting or leasing suddenly makes you realize that taking law classes might have been useful. Boring maybe, but useful. (No offense to the attorney's I know. It's just not for everyone.) IF you don't understand what you're signing do not rely on the seller / rental company to explain it to you. Get an attorney to explain the legal stuff. An informed buyer is in control of the situation and it gives you the opportunity to negotiate for other things you want.

All of these options require paper work. The volume of paperwork varies and the questions feel endless, but at the core there are some basics. Your name, current contact information, social security number, income, and credit information are the starting point. The other side will pull your credit history looking for anything that says you might not pay your bills. Additionally, they might reach out to your employer to confirm you've told them the truth about employment and you'll need money for the down payment.

Eventually you'll sit down and sign the final contract spelling out how much you will pay each month (and in total if buying) plus the length of the contract. Be sure you keep your copy of the paperwork in a safe place until a few years after you no longer live there.

Be sure you are dealing with reputable companies or you'll end up in a very bad place, starting over and dealing with a lot of painful time suckers.

IT'S ALL ABOUT YOU

There's one topic that's run through the Adulting Doesn't Have To Suck! books that we need to face head-on. You. All these tips and ideas have helped you peel back the layers of what makes you unique, then helped you make changes to improve your life. We covered maintaining your surroundings, how to manage money, even how to clean. But there is a part of you that we didn't cover. Your Health!

Breathe. I'm not a doctor and I'm not giving you medical advice. I'm going to give you mom advice. Some people seem blessed with perfect health while others struggle every day with physical or mental conditions that make life more challenging. The most important health advice anyone can give you, is that you need to pay attention to your body.

That skin bag of bones and squishy stuff walking around the house is your body. It requires food, exercise, rest, cleaning, and care. When you don't take care of your body it will stop functioning properly. Thankfully some parts of its care are easy, at least for most people.

Eat a healthy variety of foods, get some exercise, and find time to sleep every day. Right now, you can probably hear your mom telling you to eat your vegetables, go outside to play, and it's time for bed. Somewhere in there, she told you to brush your teeth, drink some water, and take a bath. Yep, mom tried to get you to build those health-important steps as you grew up.

Mom was the first person in your life helping you learn how to build good habits. These habits were the foundation for a healthy life. However, as you grew older, you chipped away at mom's advice making tweaks to fit your likes and dislikes. But some of the changes you made might have impacted your long-term health.

Did you stop brushing your teeth every day? Maybe you skip breakfast or only get about four hours of sleep most nights. Over the long-term, these changes in your basic habits have an impact on your aging body. One day you will wake up and some part of your body will make you say, Ouch!

This is the moment you need to pay attention to yourself. Knowing how you feel and how your body reacts to life helps you figure out when something isn't quite right. When something is off, you need to pay attention to the cause and effects and determine what needs to be done to correct the problem.

I'm constantly amazed by stories of people who didn't listen to their bodies until they were very sick and major damage had set in. Only you know when something is different and it's up to you to discover the reason for the change. Some things might just need a few adjustments to your habits like remembering to brush your teeth or adding some more vegetables to your diet. Others might be to add stretching, more sleep, or changes to your current exercise program to support the changes in your aging body.

Unlike your cell phone, when your body wears out, you can't trade it in for a new model. Yes, you can have surgeries to replace various things with artificial knees, hips, etc., but that not only costs a lot, but it also comes with major life disruptions.

As we get older, life and work stress, caring for children or aging parents, even changes in your hobbies all have an impact on you. Suddenly changing your sleeping and eating habits because you went from working the day shift to the night shift can be hard on the body. These are the times when you should monitor the aches and pains and assess the changes in your life that might be the cause.

So, what does all this mean? It means you need to pay attention to yourself, take care of your body, and seek input from medical professionals when things feel wrong so you can fix minor problems before they become major issues. Start paying attention today and work in the small adjustments needed to have a happy and healthier life.

PARTY TIME!

Why spend all your time cleaning and organizing if you can't show off your accomplishments? Throw a party or at least invite a few favorite friends over for a "Reinvented Me" party. You can make this as simple or complex as you'd like but remember this is to celebrate the new you.

Admit to the changes you've made based on how close the friends are. So, if you re-organized your underwear based on how much skin they covered, you might keep that between you and the BFF. But if your pantry organization now looks like a work of art, show everyone!

This section will throw out ideas to get you thinking about ways to celebrate. Nothing on the list is a *must do*. Take or toss each based on your preferences. This took work, tough decisions had to be made, and maybe a little money for you to reach the other side. The goal is to celebrate what you've accomplished and show it off. Who knows, you might inspire someone else.

Planning Is The First Step

Grab a piece of paper and let's plan a party. You need to jot down the basics to guide your steps if you want to keep this party to a level of entertaining you can enjoy.
1. Who to invite? Remember your home can't hold everyone you've ever met. Pick those who know you best and that would enjoy supporting the new you.
2. Pick a date and time. If the list of people you're inviting all play baseball on Friday nights, then don't pick a Friday during the season. Chose a time when most of them will be free and know that someone will always have a conflict.
3. The place. Easy! It's your home.
4. Eating and drinking. The core of any party is always good food. But don't make the menu so much work that you overshadow your new look with dirty dishes. If you aren't the cooking type pick stuff up from a local restaurant or make it snack stuff you can buy at the grocery store. Drinks are always a personal point of view (POV). If you don't want to serve alcohol, don't.
5. The party POV. This party is all about showing off but you can make it interactive.
    a. Ask friends to email you their favorite organizing tip before the party. Throw in one for yourself. Put each tip on an index card and challenge your friends to match the tip with the party goer. This is not only an ice breaker but you

might pick up a few more ideas along the way.
   b. Write little cards and put them up in the areas you changed with a tip on that area and what motivated you to make the adjustment.
   c. Give tours. If your bedroom was always a disaster then showing them how neat it and your closet are should be on the tour. Who knows, you might inspire others to make changes as well.
   d. Make a collage of before and after pictures and put it on a wall or a table.

Just remember this is a party to celebrate the new you. Don't let it stress you out or you'll defeat your goal of having fun.

Say Thank You

Take a moment to say an extra thank you to anyone who helped you with the transformation. You could put pictures of them helping in the areas they worked on to draw extra attention to their talents. If someone gave you a great new idea while helping be sure to give them credit.

If different friends help with each room, you could have fun making a small sign naming each area for the person and let them provide the room tour. (Betty's Blue Bathroom, Sam's Spicy Red Kitchen, or even Pat's Relaxing Patio Playroom.) Encourage your friends to brag about how they helped you and announce what you plan to do in return.

If you have a bit of extra cash, you could also buy them a small thank you gift. It can be small things like a gift card for their favorite restaurant, a massage gift certificate, or a home accessory they want. If you don't have a lot of cash, make gift cards for each that can be redeemed for things you can do for them. Ideas include helping them with a room makeover at their house, washing their car, or cooking them dinner. Sometimes these are the best gifts a friend can get. Just be sure they know you appreciate the help they provided and say thank you several times.

And I'd like to say *Thank You* to the people in my life who encouraged me to write my Adulting Doesn't Have To Suck! books, gave me ideas and tips to make life easier, and to my mom who tried to teach me how to take care of myself (miss you). You've all played a part in shaping who I am and how I deal with life.

To my readers, thank you for buying my books. I hope they've inspired you to make changes that makes life better for you. Don't forget to post a review letting me know which tips were your favorite and share one of your own. You're never too old to learn from tips you get from others, even me.

Thank you. Thank you. *Thank you!*

APPENDIX - How To Make A Box

Many people made Fortune Teller paper toys when they were growing up, especially the girls. We folded the paper, filled in the answers to questions about boys, and played fortune teller with our friends for hours. Folding the paper and slipping in your fingers to make it move made you a genius among your peers. You created the cool toy.

Making a box takes your abilities to the next level with something that is functional and decorative. It's not very hard. Make your first box out of some copier paper or newspaper if you're worried about wasting the good paper. Let's get started.

There are two separate parts of the box – the top and the bottom. If you want to make them more decorative, use a solid color paper for the bottom and a patterned paper for the top. Slightly stiff paper like wrapping paper, scrap book paper, or light weight cover stocks work best. My boxes end up as approximately two-inch squares.

Adjust the finished size by starting with a larger or smaller square. Each piece is built the same way with the only difference being the difference in the size of the starting pieces. I've drawn lines on these examples to help you understand how to make the folds. You don't need to draw any lines on your boxes. I've provided pictures to help you see the steps.

Start by measuring and cutting out a square piece of paper for each part.
- Bottom – cut a 5" x 5" square
- Top – cut a 5 ½" x 5 ½" square

Fold the point of each corner of a square into the center. The points of each corner should touch in the center but don't let the edges overlap.

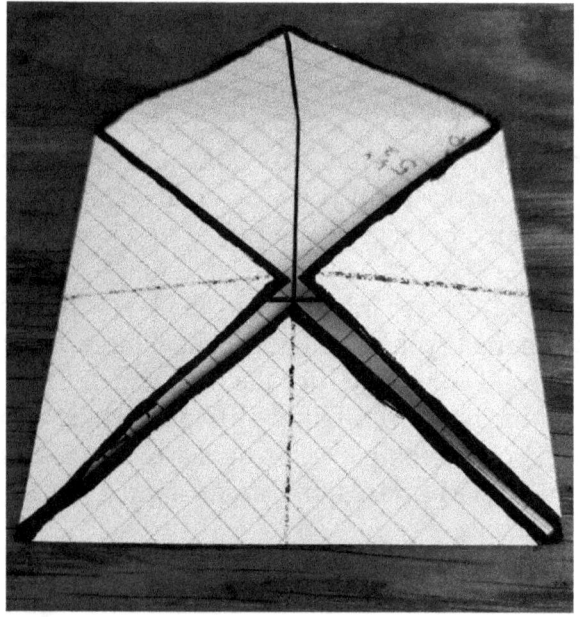

Next, we want to create some lines that will help with the needed cuts and form the center bottom. Fold the long sides into the middle hiding your points.

Appendix - How To Make A Box | 203

Open those back out and make the same folds from the other direction. When you've finished all the folds you might find the points popping up in the center. It's okay and actually very helpful. You'll see a natural square in the center of the box. That will become the bottom so you know what size the finished piece will become.

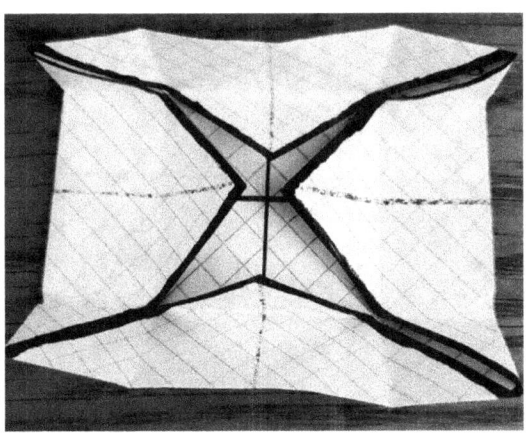

Now you'll pick a set of flaps (A & B) opposite of each other to be the ones we'll cut. These cuts will make fold flaps that will form the sides.

Open out flap A and make a cut down the long line until you reach the center square (dotted line) that will make up the bottom of the box. Don't cut into that square. (Look at the picture.)

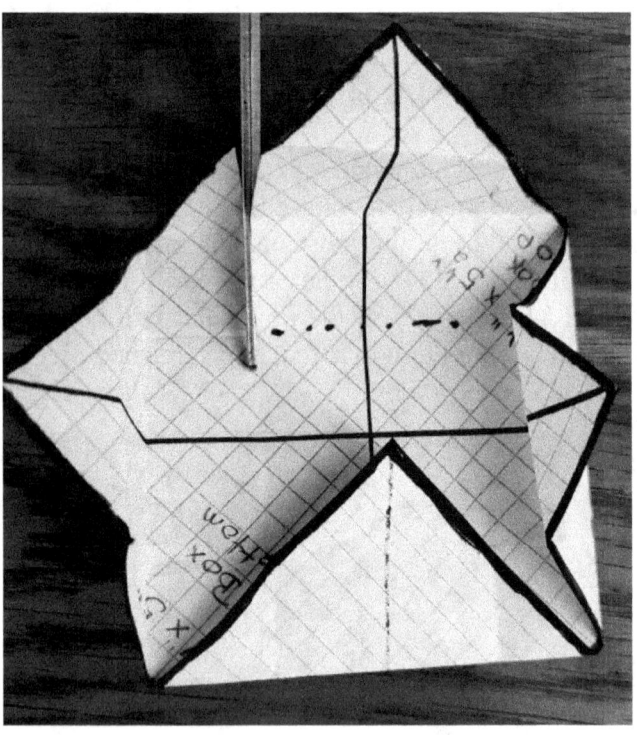

Make the cuts on both sides of each (A & B) key flaps. It's a total of four cuts. The points of these flaps will end up on the bottom of your box.

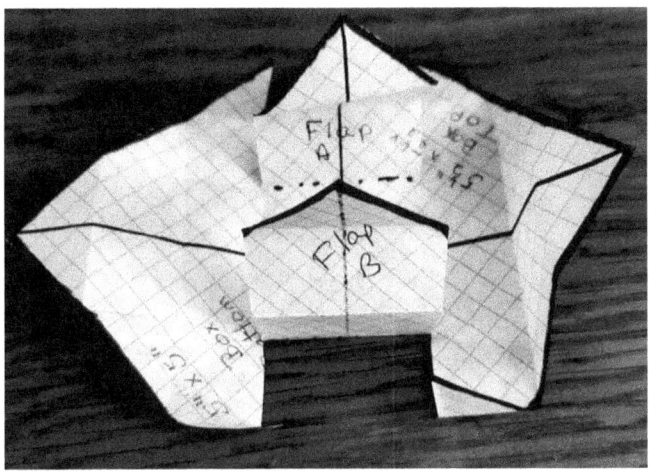

Pulling the key flaps (A & B) toward the center will allow little wings on the sides to stand out. (Those small tips fold in on themselves forming a square to stiffen the side and be hidden under the flaps.) Pull the side pieces in front of the key flaps. You should be able to see the square that forms the bottom and these folded in will look like sides. Now you need to secure the sides.

Fold flap A over the top of the wing flaps. Tuck it back flat to form one side with the point sitting on the bottom and the fold line hitting on the edge of the box bottom. Repeat with side B.

Ta Da! You now have a box. Pinching the outside of the box along the bottom square lines will tighten the fit and tighten the box shape. You can put glue on the flaps to hold them down but part of the fun is allowing others to unfold the box and be inspired to make their own. Glued flaps don't support that.

The weight of the paper you select dictates the amount of pressure needed to make the edges crisp. The heavier the stock the more you will want to crease the folds at each step.

Now follow the steps again to make the top and before you know it, you have a cool box.

Experiment with special occasion, holiday wrapping paper, even scrap booking paper. The boxes are great for a variety of things like holding earring backers and safety pins or wrapping up special gifts like jewelry or money. (Yeah, money!)

Happy Box Making!

Dear Reader,

If you enjoyed Adulting Doesn't Have To Suck! or Adulting Doesn't Have To Suck! #2, please take a moment to leave a review on your favorite book or social media site. And if you have an organizing or cleaning tip, share those on my website or social media sites. I look forward to reading them!

Thank you,

Pat Sawtelle
www.PatSawtelle.com

Works available by Pat Sawtelle

Short Stories
Caffeine Moon
My First Wolf Moon
The Fairy's Kiss
The Feathered Crown
The Key

Chalice Princess Novel Series
Chalice Moon

Non-Fiction
Adulting Doesn't Have To Suck!
Adulting Doesn't Have To Suck! #2

www.ingramcontent.com/pod-product-compliance
Lightning Source LLC
Chambersburg PA
CBHW071431070526
44578CB00001B/65